PREFACE

When I say to the wicked, 'You shall surely die,' and you give him no warning, nor speak to warn the wicked from his wicked way, to save his life, that same wicked man shall die in his iniquity; but his blood I will require at your hand. Yet, if you warn the wicked, and he does not turn from his wickedness, nor from his wicked way, he shall die in his iniquity; but you have delivered your soul. "Again, when a righteous man turns from his righteousness and commits iniquity, and I lay a stumbling block before him, he shall die; because you did not give him warning, he shall die in his sin, and his righteousness which he has done shall not be remembered; but his blood I will require at your hand. Nevertheless if you warn the righteous man that the righteous should not sin, and he does not sin, he shall surely live because he took warning; also you will have delivered your soul." (Ezekiel 3:18-21)

IN THEIR OWN WORDS

*"Laws have to be backed up with resources and political will. And **deep-seated** cultural codes, **religious beliefs** and structural biases **have to be changed"*- Hillary Clinton April 23, 2015 (Ertelt, 2015).

Hillary Clinton suggesting that the force of law should be used to compel Christians to embrace the murder of unborn children (abortion).

"A Democratic ticket is the clear ticket that we should be voting on, regardless of who said what or did this– that shouldn't even come into the equation." ***"Don't think, just vote democrat"*** Michelle Obama 2014 (Hunter, 2014).

Michelle Obama instructing blacks to put aside their God given ability to think and reason and to support democrats regardless of their characters or policy results.

"Hire three or more colored ministers, preferably with social service backgrounds, and with engaging personalities." ***"We do not want word to get out that we want to exterminate the Negro population, and the minister is the man who can straighten out that idea if it ever occurs to any of their more rebellious members"*** (Drogin, 1989, p. 25).

Excerpt from a letter written by Planned Parenthood founder Margaret Sanger outlining her plan to exterminate blacks.

THOUGH THEY SLAY US,
STILL WILL WE TRUST THEM

THOUGH THEY SLAY US,
STILL WILL WE TRUST THEM

*Are Black Christians More Obedient to the
Democrat Party than to Christ?*

MARK LINEN

THOUGH THEY SLAY US,
STILL WILL WE TRUST THEM

World Ahead Press is a division of WND Books. The views and opinions expressed in this book are those of the author and do not necessarily reflect the official policy or position or WND Books.
Unless otherwise noted, Scripture quotations are taken from THE NEW KING JAMES VERSION. © 1982 by Thomas Nelson, Inc. Used by permission. All rights reserved.

Paperback ISBN: 978-1-944212-26-1
eBook ISBN: 978-1-944212-27-8

Printed in the United States of America
16 17 18 19 20 21 LSI 9 8 7 6 5 4 3 2 1

CONTENTS

CHAPTER 1

TAUGHT TO BELIEVE A LIE

"The coming of the lawless one is according to the working of Satan, with all power, signs, and lying wonders, and with all unrighteous deception among those who perish, because they did not receive the love of the truth, that they might be saved. And for this reason God will send them strong delusion, that they should believe the lie, that they all may be condemned who did not believe the truth but had pleasure in unrighteousness." (2 Thess. 2:9–12)

COLOR OVER CHRIST
AND POLITICS OVER PRINCIPLES

You have wearied the Lord with your words; Yet you say, "In
what way have we wearied Him?" In that you say, "Everyone
who does evil Is good in the sight of the Lord, And He delights
in them," Or, "Where is the God of justice?"
(Mal. 2:17)

After the election of Barack Hussein Obama (BHO), many political pundits insinuated that blacks had voted for Obama simply because he was a black man. That, however, was not really the case. Nearly 90 percent of blacks will consistently cast their votes for Democrats.[1] It is not that we share the anti-Christian vison that those on the left have for our country. A vision of a Christless society, a society where the lives of the unborn are counted as worthless, where their bodies are seen as good for nothing but to be chopped up and sold to the highest bidder.

The left desire a society where deviant sexual practices are to be celebrated and where any opposition to those practices will not be tolerated. Most black Christians, those of my generation and older, believe that Christians should be free to practice their faith without government interference. Most are against the brutal and barbaric murder of unborn children, and the great majority view marriage as the union of a man and a woman. And yet, through emotional manipulation, lies, and half-truths about history, biased media coverage, and the treachery of so-called black leaders, these are the very things that we support, bringing to mind Romans 7:15–19. Not too long ago I was no different; however, I had to decide whether my loyalties would be to Christ or to the Democrats.

For nearly 90 percent of blacks, political affiliation trumps skin color, morality, the well- being of our children and our faith. In heated debates with some of these precious people all have admitted, that regardless of democrat policies that run contrary to scripture, they would unconditionally support democrats. More on that later. In 2008, BHO received 96 percent of the black vote.[2] However, I do agree that there were some who voted for BHO simply because of the color of his skin. Even some black Republicans, once thought to be men of character and principle, have abandoned their stated values to vote for a man simply because of the color of his skin. In *Why Black Republicans Support Obama*, the Reverend Jesse Lee Peterson identifies some well-known black Republicans who were either considering, or determined to vote for BHO. It would seem that these "conservatives" and evangelicals care more about BHO's skin color than about his record.

BHO has promoted the murder of the unborn via abortion like no one before him. He has thrown the full weight of the White House behind redefining the God-ordained institution of marriage, equating it with those acts practiced by the citizens of Sodom and Gomorrah, and he would have Christians worship according to the will of Obama and not the precepts of Christ. And yet, these conservatives and Christians, J. C. Watts and Armstrong Williams, seemed rather infatuated with BHO.

According to findbiography.org (2016), in 1990 J. C. Watts, a Republican, became the first black man elected to statewide office in Oklahoma. Mr. Watts was elected to the U. S. House of Representatives in 1994. The author contends that Mr. Watts was the first black congressman who did not join the Congressional Black Caucus.

In 1997, Mr. Watts delivered the Republican Party's response to then President Bill Clinton's State of the Union Address. In His response, Mr. Watts accused black Democrats of being "race-hustling poverty pimps" whose livelihoods depended on keeping blacks dependent on the government (Findbiography, 2016). Armstrong Williams is a longtime conservative journalist and author who was mentored by the late Senator Strom Thurmond (Ross, 2016). According to Ross (2016), Williams once stated that his family had been Republicans ever since the Lincoln presidency. Most recently, Mr. Williams was known as the top adviser to Dr. Ben Carson's now-suspended presidential campaign. How surprising that two such normally well-informed men would even consider jumping ship to promote the very things that they had spoken out against for years.

T. D. Jakes, a well-known black mega church pastor who in the past supported conservative presidential candidates, seemed to be enamored with the idea of a BHO presidency. Reverend Jakes said that a victory for BHO would be a victory for African Americans.[3] But, after serving (perhaps *dictating* or *ruling* would be better words) for nearly eight years now, it would seem that this victory for Obama has instead been a victory for Islamic terrorists, those who murder the unborn, those who practice the lifestyle of Sodom and Gomorrah (homosexuality), and, of course, a tremendous victory for the Iranian regime.

And then there was General Colin Powell, former Secretary of State under President George W. Bush. Powell has proven himself to be a Republican in the mold of Arlen Specter, the late senator from Pennsylvania who changed his party affiliation from Republican to Democrat to get on the Obama bandwagon. Mr. Powell was at first evasive when asked if he would support fellow Republican John McCain or Democrat BHO for the presidency in the 2004 presidential election. As BHO gained momentum, Mr. Powell could no longer contain himself and, casting aside any semblance of indecision, lent his support to BHO.[4]

In a classic case of the law of the harvest, sowing and reaping, General Powell did to Senator McCain what McCain had made a career of doing to members of his own party, which McCain had proudly boasted of on so many occasions as "crossing the aisle to work with the other side."

Reverend Jakes, Representative J. C. Watts, Armstrong Williams,[5] and General Colin Powell, I think, represent only a small number of those blacks who actually may have voted for BHO based on the color of his skin. Unfortunately for most in the black community, however, the only requirement for our votes is that the candidate label himself a "Democrat."

On the other hand, I do believe that many more whites than blacks voted for BHO because of the color of his skin. Although I have no statistics to support this theory, I suspect that many white Americans, weary of being branded racist and eager to prove that America is not a racist country, embraced the chance of making history and electing America's first black president. In a nationally televised interview Pastor Joel Osteen and his wife declared that they thought BHO was doing a great job,[6] all while BHO was increasing the murder of unborn babies (abortion) and launching attack after attack at the God-ordained institution of marriage. After BHO's election, a white friend who supported him stated that he hoped the election of BHO would put an end to the claims that America is a racist nation. I warned him that, based on some of BHO's pre-election speeches, those claims would in all likelihood only increase. I'm sad to say that I was right, as this man whom many expected would unify the nation has instead divided it.

This post-racial president has become, as author Mark Tapson wrote, the "most-racial president." The unconditional support of the black community for the Democrat Party defies logic. Blacks are the nation's most religious group,[7] yet the Democrats are champions of secularism and are always laying the groundwork to make our faith in Christ more difficult to practice, at best, and illegal, at worst.

The Democrats ferociously support the goals of Planned Parenthood, perhaps the most prolific murderers of unborn children in the history of the world. Planned Parenthood was founded by Margaret Sanger for the specific purpose of exterminating the black race. The website TooManyAborted uses Sanger's own words to illustrate her views on poor and minority populations, citing statements from articles and books authored by Sanger.

For instance, Sanger lays out her plans for dealing with the unfit and segregated populations in *Birth Control Review*, "Plan for Peace," April 1932, Vol 26, Number 4, as well as her book *Pivot of Civilization* (Chapter V, "Cruelty of Charity" and chapter 18, "Women and the New Race"), and the article "Birth Control and Racial Betterment" from *Birth Control Review*, Feb 1919, p. 11.

Author Tanya Green illustrates Sanger's plans for exterminating blacks by citing a letter she, Sanger, wrote to Clarence Gamble, regional director of the south's Birth Control Federation of America (BCFA). In the December, 1939, letter Sanger discussed her plans to use black pastors to convince blacks to participate in their own extermination. Sanger wrote,

> *The minister's work is also important and he should be trained, perhaps by the Federation as to our ideals and the goal that we hope to reach. We do not want word to go out that we want to exterminate the Negro population, and the minister is the man who can straighten out that idea if it ever occurs to any of their more rebellious members.*

Then, as it is now, black leaders were, and are, crucial to progressing the goals of Planned Parenthood.

And, while we black Christians claim to be against the lifestyle of Sodom and Gomorrah and the murder of unborn children, we are the most loyal supporters of those who advocate for both—the Democrat Party.

HE WHO FIRST PRESENTS HIS CASE

"The first one to plead his cause seems right,
until his neighbor comes and examines him"
(Prov. 18:17).

Blacks' support for those who are destroying them and corrupting their children is indeed baffling. When one examines this situation through the lens of the biblical truth, however, it becomes easier to understand. From an early age, blacks are taught that Democrats are "looking out for us," whereas Republicans are racists who seek a return to the days of Jim Crow. We are taught that the Republican Party supported and encouraged slavery in the early days of the country. *The first one to plead his cause seems right, until his neighbor comes and examines him* (Prov. 18:17). This verse states that people tend to believe the first side of a story that they hear. And since we blacks typically refuse so much as to listen to the second side, the side of the opposing party, we are left believing the accounts of those on the left. And as a people we have demonstrated to the Democrats that no matter how badly they treat us, ignore us, and take us for granted, we will still support them.

I often say that racists, those who have already made up their mind about a person based solely on the color of that person's skin, are cheating themselves out of some potentially rewarding relationships. I think that the same applies to those who refuse to hear all opposing sides of the political debate.

Because they know that the black community will support them regardless of how negatively their actions affect us, the Democrats no longer seek to disguise their goals. As Proverbs 1:17 says, they have laid the trap out in plain sight, and we have willingly rushed into it, with our quality of life and our children and their potential in tow.[8]

When Senator John Kerry was running for president, he told the black community, in *politicalese*, that he was going to encourage our children to embrace sexual deviancy (homosexuality). While claiming to support biblical marriage, obviously for political expediency; he, ironically, opposed the Defense of Marriage Act. When discussing judicial appointments, Kerry indicated that he would ensure that the murder of our unborn not only be continued but increased if he had anything to say about it by only appointing judges that believed it was a right to murder babies before they are born, and that he would make sure that our children remained in the worst-performing schools that the nation has to offer by opposing school choice and voucher programs.[9] And we blacks applauded him as we commented on how presidential he looked and sounded. *"Son of man, thou dwellest in the midst of a rebellious house, which have eyes to see, and see not; they have ears to hear, and hear not: for they are a rebellious house"* (Ezek. 12:2).

"And through covetousness shall they with feigned words make merchandise of you: whose judgment now of a long time lingereth not, and their damnation slumbereth not" (2 Peter 2:3).

The treatment of blacks by the Democrat Party is far worse than merely taking them for granted. They have used us like a product. The product we provide for them is our votes and the lives and futures of our young. In return, we get empty rhetoric each election season. Even traitorous Judas received something of value.

Throughout the nation it is largely Republicans who are fighting for such issues as school choice and school vouchers. These programs would give blacks the option of taking their children out of failing, under-performing, and violent schools. It is largely Republicans who are fighting to restrict or end the brutal practice of murdering unborn babies (abortion)—a practice that has taken a terrible toll on the nation, especially on the black community. And it is Republicans who are fighting to prevent the entire nation from becoming a modern-day version of Sodom and Gomorrah, as state after state, and even the military, have begun to embrace the lifestyle that Scripture calls "vile" (Judges 19:24), "wicked" (Gen. 19:7) and an "abomination" (Lev. 18:22). And while the Republicans are fighting for causes that the black community says it supports, those on the left, led by the Democrat Party, are committed to keeping our children in failing schools meant only to indoctrinate, not to educate. The Democrats are fighting to keep Planned Parenthood founder Margaret Sanger's vision for the black community alive. They are doing everything in their considerable power to increase the spread of deviant sexual behavior until the entire nation is a reflection of the cities of Sodom and Gomorrah, which elicited God's wrath.

Kelly Williams-Bolar, a single black mother, was jailed recently for having the initiative to seek and pursue a good education for her two daughters. This woman who lived in a housing project in Akron, Ohio, used her father's address in order to send her children to another school district where they would get a quality education. Convicted of falsifying records so that her children could receive a better education, she was not only jailed, but because of the conviction her dreams of becoming a teacher were put in jeopardy.[10] One would think that those who claim to have the best interests of blacks in mind, Democrats, and especially the Congressional Black Caucus, would come out in support of this courageous woman. No such luck. In fact, it is the policies of the Democrat Party that have condemned blacks to the very types of schools that Ms. Williams-Bolar was trying to remove her daughters from.

WOUNDED IN THE HOUSE OF MY FRIENDS

And one will say to him, 'What are these wounds between your arms?' Then he will answer, 'Those with which I was wounded in the house of my friends
(Zech. 13:6).

As a boy growing up, I was led to believe that the "peculiar institution" of slavery was promoted and defended by the Republicans. And even today I frequently hear some of my fellows mouth the words that "the Republicans want to take us back to the times of slavery." It wasn't until much later in life that I learned the truth that it was instead the Democrats who were the brutal slave masters.[11] During that time period Democrats justified the inhumane, degrading, brutal treatment and ownership of blacks with the claim that blacks were not people. This same denial of personhood was later used by Adolf Hitler to justify the murder of millions of Jews and is used today to justify the murder of millions of unborn (and until recently newly born) babies. Season after season, Satan continues to use this same tactic, the denial of personhood, to great effect. They insisted that slavery was the natural state of the black man who could not otherwise survive because he was naturally inferior, a theme they continue to support through their opposition to voter ID laws, the insinuation being that minorities are not intelligent enough to simply provide proof of identity. A Pennsylvania judge, in striking down that state's voter ID law, ruled that providing an ID was just too much of a burden for minorities.[12]

During the Civil War, Democrats were willing to put their lives on the line in order to preserve their ownership of blacks and the state-sanctioned right to murder, mutilate, brutalize, and rape blacks. The Republican Party's origins, on the other hand, were founded on the opposition to slavery. And just as the Democrats were willing to give their lives to keep blacks in a condition lower than that of the family dog, the Republicans were willing to give their lives so that blacks could have the freedom and dignity of all those created in the image of God.

During the Civil War, freed blacks and former slaves joined the Union armies and provided the extra manpower that was the deciding factor in the Union victory.[6] Although the Thirteenth Amendment abolished slavery, however, thanks exclusively to the efforts of Democrats, freed blacks soon found that there was very little difference between freedom and slavery. Even though the federal government instituted the Freedmen's Bureau to assist recently freed slaves with relocation, education, and other supplies necessary for survival, most blacks were still poor and illiterate—conditions that the Democrats quickly exploited. Determined to continue the inhumane practice of slavery by any means necessary, the Democrats soon devised other methods to keep blacks in positions of servitude.

Refusing to give the black man his freedom and dignity, the Southern Democrats continued the practice of slavery, only now they disguised it through a series of restrictions on blacks that came to be known as the "Black Codes." The Black Codes were laws passed by Democrats in the Southern states that placed restrictions on blacks' civil rights. The Black Codes seemed to be a resurrection of the old slave codes, placing some of the same restrictions on free blacks that were placed on the slaves. For instance, these codes limited or prohibited blacks from owning land, limited their right to testify against white men, prohibited them from owning weapons, and prohibited them from learning skilled trades.[13] The Black Codes, including its vagrancy laws and apprentice laws, combined with the practice of share cropping, which effectively bound a family to a plantation owner, threatened to nullify any benefits that freedom and Republican President Abraham Lincoln's Emancipation Proclamation should have bestowed on blacks.

Recognizing these Black Codes for what they were—the continuation of slavery—Thaddeus Stevens and the Radical Republicans gained congressional approval for the Civil Rights Act of 1866, which gave blacks the rights and privileges of full citizenship.[14]

Stevens and the Radical Republicans followed up by proposing the Fourteenth Amendment, which granted citizenship to blacks and guaranteed that all federal and state laws applied equally to blacks and whites. The amendment also barred former Confederate federal and state office holders from ever holding political office again. Stevens and the Republicans declared that no Southern state would be readmitted to the Union until the Fourteenth Amendment was ratified.

Thanks exclusively to the efforts of Thaddeus Stevens and the Radical Republicans, who were fought every step of the way by President Andrew Johnson, who believed blacks were inferior and should have remained slaves, blacks were registered to vote, and were legally afforded the same rights as white citizens.[15]

Thaddeus Stevens was totally devoted to the freedom of blacks, and at his death he further expressed his unity with blacks by choosing to be laid to rest in an all-black cemetery.[16] The newly gained political power of the emancipated blacks led to Hiram Revels' election as the first black US Senator in 1870 and to the election of black representatives Benjamin S. Turner, Josiah T. Walls, Robert Brown Elliot, Robert D. De Large, Jefferson H. Long, and Georgetown, South Carolina's own Joseph H. Rainey, who was the first black man to be seated in the US House of Representatives.

During this period, known as Reconstruction, which lasted from 1865 to 1877, blacks went from being slaves to being elected to local, state, and national offices.

Democrats remained reluctant to give up their barbaric hold on blacks, and what they could not achieve through legal means they sought to achieve through voter fraud, efforts designed to take advantage of most blacks' lack of education. Along with voter fraud, the Democrats also resorted to intimidation and violence through white supremacist terrorist groups, chief among them the notorious Ku Klux Klan (KKK).

Although federal troops were deployed to the Southern states to secure the rights of freed blacks, Democrats continued to gain power through voter fraud, violence, and intimidation. Once again politically relevant, during a bitter dispute of the presidential vote of 1876, Democrats were able to forge a compromise with the Republicans in which the Republican candidate, Rutherford B. Hayes, would be declared the winner in return for the federal government's withdrawing troops from the Southern states. This compromise, the Compromise of 1877, along with the Supreme Court's 1883 ruling that deemed the Civil Rights Act of 1875 unconstitutional, and, chiefly, the determination of the Democrats to maintain their control over blacks, would serve to set the black community back for untold years, as blacks went from holding political and legal offices to social enslavement, being free men in name only.[17]

Thanks to Thaddeus Stevens and the Radical Republicans, blacks enjoyed a measure of freedom and influence during Reconstruction. But the Compromise of 1877 ended reconstruction and Southern Democrats resurrected some aspects of the Black Codes through the institution of Jim Crow laws. It would not be until the passage of the Civil Rights Act of 1964 that blacks would be free from the injustices of Jim Crow.[18]

Through the years, however, Republicans continued to fight for the civil rights of blacks, despite the opposition of Democrats, and blacks continued to support the Republicans, the party of Lincoln.

Owing to a series of events, Republicans lost the black vote. During the Great Depression, Democrat FDR's anti-poverty and work programs cast him in a favorable light among blacks. But the major exodus of blacks from the Republican Party occurred during the civil rights struggles of the mid-1960s. Someone once said that "perception is everything." When Democratic President Lyndon Baines Johnson and a Congress in which Democrats were a majority passed the Civil Rights Act of 1964 and the 1965 Voting Rights Act, the perception was that Democrats had achieved a major victory for the civil rights of blacks. Further strengthening the misguided perception that Democrats now had the best interests of blacks at heart was Republican Barry Goldwater's opposition to the Civil Rights Act as it was written.[19]

The unseen reality was that both pieces of legislation were authored by Republicans and in previous years had been blocked by the Democrats. In 1957 Republican President Dwight D. Eisenhower authored the Civil Rights Act, an updated version of Radical Republican Charles Sumner's 1875 Civil Rights Act, in an effort to return to blacks the rights that Democrats had rescinded after the end of Reconstruction. In 1960, Republican Senator Everett Dirksen authored a voting rights bill seeking to outlaw the Jim Crow laws that Democrats used to restrict and prohibit blacks from voting. Senator Dirksen's Voting Rights Act would have made poll taxes, literacy tests, and the violence and intimidation used by the original terrorists, the KKK, unlawful. But just as they had done with Eisenhower's Civil Rights Act, the Democrats opposed Senator Dirksen's bill.[20]

Also unseen, or perhaps merely ignored, was that the Democrat majority opposed both pieces of legislation. Democrats launched a fifty-seven-day filibuster in their attempts to block passage of the 1964 Civil Rights Act. Al Gore Sr. refused to vote on the legislation. Former Klansman Democrat Senator Robert Byrd (who died in 2010 while still serving in the Senate) sought to stop passage by conducting a 14-hour 13-minute filibuster.[21] But despite the Democrats' opposition and maneuvering, the Republicans once again won another round in the battle for equality for blacks.

Today, Democrats continue to portray themselves as champions of the civil rights of blacks while painting the Republicans, who for some reason refuse to defend their history, as racists and champions of segregation. History, however, tells a different story. Scripture tells us that there is nothing new under the sun: *"That which has been is what will be, that which is done is what will be done, and there is nothing new under the sun"* (Eccl. 1:9).

Today the Democrats still restrict blacks' opportunities for a quality education, and would tell us how we are to worship and what our pastors can and cannot say, and they oppose every measure aimed at preventing the slaughter of our unborn children.

A speech that Joseph Rainey of Georgetown, South Carolina, one of the first black congressmen in the United States, made in 1871 reads as if it were spoken in modern times. This speech was in response to negative remarks that a Democratic representative from New York made about black members of the South Carolina state legislature. Rainey said:

The remarks made by the gentleman from New York in relation to the colored people of South Carolina escaped my hearing, as I was in the rear of the Hall when they were made, and I did not know that any utterance of that kind had emanated from him. I have always entertained a high regard for the gentleman from New York, because I believed him to be a useful member of the House. He is a gentleman of talent and of fine education, and I have thought heretofore that he would certainly be charitable toward a race of people who have never enjoyed the same advantages that he has. If the colored people of South Carolina had been accorded the same advantages—if they had had the same wealth and surroundings which the gentleman from New York has had, they would have shown to this nation that their color was no obstacle to their holding positions of trust, political or otherwise. Not having had these advantages, we cannot at the present time compete with the favored race of this country;

but perhaps if our lives are spared, and if the gentleman from New York and other gentlemen on that side of the House will only accord to us right and justice, we shall show to them that we can be useful, intelligent citizens of this country. But if they will continue to proscribe us, if they will continue to cultivate prejudice against us; if they will continue to decry the Negro and crush him under foot, then **you cannot expect the Negro to rise while the Democrats are trampling upon him and his rights***. We ask you, sir, to do by the Negro as you ought to do by him in justice.*

If the Democrats are such staunch friends of the Negro, why is it that when propositions are offered here and elsewhere looking to the elevation of the colored race, and the extension of right and justice to them, do the Democrats array themselves in unbroken phalanx, and vote against every such measure? *You, gentlemen of that side of the House, have voted against all the recent amendments of the Constitution, and the laws enforcing the same. Why did you do it? I answer, because those measures had a tendency to give to the poor Negro his just rights, and because they proposed to knock off his shackles and give him* **freedom of speech, freedom of action, and the opportunity of education, that he might elevate himself to the dignity of manhood.**

Now **you come to us and say that you are our best friends***. We would that we could look upon you as such. We would that your votes as recorded in the Globe from day to day could only demonstrate it. But your votes, your actions, and the constant cultivation of your cherished prejudices prove to the Negroes of the entire country that the Democrats are in opposition to them, and if they [the Democrats] could have sway our race would have no foothold here. Now, sir, I have not time to vindicate fully the course of action* *of the colored people of South Carolina. We are certainly in the majority there; I admit that we are as two to one. Sir, I ask this House, I ask the country, I ask white men, I ask Democrats, I ask Republicans whether the Negroes have presumed to take improper advantage of the majority they hold in that State by disregarding the interest of the minority? They have not. Our convention which met in 1868, and in which the Negroes were in a large majority, did not pass any proscriptive or disfranchising acts, but adopted a liberal constitution, securing alike equal rights to all citizens, white and black, male and female, as far as possible. Mark you, we did not discriminate, although we had a majority. Our constitution towers up in its majesty with provisions for equal protection of all classes and citizens. Notwithstanding our majority there, we have never attempted to deprive any man in that State of the rights and immunities to which he is entitled under the Constitution of this Government. You cannot point me to a single act passed by our Legislature, at any time, which had a tendency to reflect upon or oppress any white citizen of South Carolina. You cannot show me one enactment by which the majority in our State have undertaken to crush the white men because the latter are in a minority.*

I say to you, gentlemen of the Democratic party, that I want you to deal justly with the people composing my race. I am here representing a Republican constituency made up of white and colored men. I say to you deal with us justly; be charitable toward us. An opportunity will soon present itself when we can test whether you on that side of the House are the best friends of the oppressed and ill-treated Negro race. When the civil rights bill comes before you, when that bill comes up upon its merits asking you to give civil rights of the Negro, I will then see who are our best friends on that side of the House.

"I will say to the gentleman from New York that I am sorry I am constrained to make these remarks. I wish to say to him that I do not mind what he may have said against the Negroes of South Carolina. Neither his friendship nor his enmity will change the sentiment of the loyal men of that State. We are determined to stand by this Government. We are determined to use judiciously and wisely the prerogative conferred upon us by the Republican party. **The Democratic party may woo us, they may court us and try to get us to worship at their shrine,** *but I will tell the gentleman that we are Republicans by instinct, and we will be Republicans so long as God will allow our proper senses to hold sway over us"*[22] (emphasis mine).

CRY RACISM

"He who hates, disguises it with his lips, and lays up deceit
within himself; when he speaks kindly, do not believe him, for
there are seven abominations in his heart; though his hatred is
covered by deceit, His wickedness will be revealed
before the assembly"
(Prov. 26:24–26).

I t's almost understandable that one could be misled about events
that happened so long ago, but there is no excuse in today's
information age to believe the lies that today's politicians spew
forth. Democrats will completely ignore the state and needs of blacks
until election season rolls around when, without fail, they come out
and begin making claims of racism against the opposition party.
Once again, effectively implying that blacks and other minorities
are not intelligent enough to provide proof of identity at voting
polls, Hillary Clinton, as she campaigns for the 2016 presidential
election, has begun accusing Republican candidates of trying to
prevent minorities from voting.[23] Just as sure as death and taxes are
inevitable, so too is the assurance that Democrats will cry racism to
mobilize blacks before, during, and after elections.

When people opposed BHO's signature piece of healthcare
reform legislation—the Affordable Care Act, known commonly as
Obamacare—the Democrats, as expected, began making claims that
those who opposed it did so simply because Obama was black. The
truth is that many, such as myself, were and are against Obamacare

because in addition to the fact that we simply don't know enough about it, we don't feel that the government should have the power to force anyone to purchase insurance and because the manner in which it was passed reeked of bribery (Montopoli, 2009) and deception, now confirmed by Jonathon Gruber (Thiessen, 2014). And because the actions of many of those on the Democrat side seemed to support the allegations of pro-life groups that the legislation would be used to increase the taxpayer-funded murder of unborn babies (abortions).

In 2002, when Mississippi judge Charles Pickering was nominated to the 5th US Circuit Court of Appeals, the Democrats trotted out Julian Bond and the NAACP to declare that Pickering was a racist of the worst kind—this while those blacks who actually knew judge Pickering, those who lived in Mississippi, had nothing but praise for the man.[24]

When members of the Tea Party demanded smaller government, lower taxes, and an end to wasteful spending, out came the NAACP to make their baseless claims of racism. When the liberal Democrats cannot win an argument based on the merits (and they seldom can), when they don't want to hear any reasonable opposition (and they never do), they resort to claims of racism and most of the opposing voices go silent.

The words *racism* and *racist* are perhaps the most powerful words in American society. The racism accusation (also known as playing the race card) has been so effective in our society that Jack McMahon, the attorney representing mass child murderer Kermit Gosnell, MD, did not hesitate to use it as the reason for murder charges being filed against his client. Gosnell, the poster child for all who claim to be pro-choice (pro death), was another "doctor" who didn't have what it takes to save lives and thus resorted to taking them instead. Lacking the diabolical skills to properly legally murder the child before birth, he took to delivering them alive and then cutting their spinal cords. It speaks volumes about the state of our society that his attorney would even voice racism as a defense.[25]

I suspect the fear of being called racist is what prevents those with legitimate concerns about Obama's eligibility to hold the office of president from speaking out and restrains those who have questions about his Social Security number from probing further. According to democrat and republican alike, it is somehow racist to question BHO's birthplace. It matters not that it was BHO himself who, in the printed biography for the books that he would write, stated that he was in fact born in Kenya and raised in Indonesia and Hawaii. (Farah, 2016). And now, suddenly, it is racist to expect males to use male restrooms and females to use female restrooms. Demonstrating that she is more than an adequate replacement for the corrupt, professional racist Eric Holder, Attorney General Loretta Lynch has compared all opposition to allowing males in female restrooms with the racist Jim Crow Laws (Richter, 2016). If allowed to stand, I suspect that this law will give males access to not only female restrooms but also their dorm rooms and showers. In this day and age when it is dangerous to allow underage boys to go to restrooms unaccompanied, now BHO wants to give sexual predators access to our loved ones in department stores, restaurants, libraries, dorm rooms and showers. After thousands of years of their being only males and females (*So God created man in His own image; in the image of God He created him;* **male and female** *He created them -* Gen. 1:27) those on the left have created a third gender, transgender, once again pointing out that they know better than the Creator.

Democrats have learned that all they need do to silence their opposition is simply lie about the past and make claims of racism in the present. That way they can get us to behave exactly as they want us to. Some years ago a friend who served as a substitute teacher from time to time told me of a class of students at an all-black school which demanded candy in order to behave. One white instructor accommodated them by giving them candy in return for behaving. When my friend was called upon to exchange candy for good behavior, she explained to the class that this was the same method that animal trainers used to get animals to do what they wanted them to do. After that, she said, the students became ashamed and vowed to behave without the promise of rewards.

This scenario is similar to the relationship between blacks and the Democrat Party except that while those students were able to extract something from their white instructor—candy—the black community gets nothing in return from the Democrats. To the contrary, while our votes may benefit the citizens of Mexico and the homosexual community, for over fifty years the black community has gotten nothing.

Is it any wonder that claims of racism seem to spike during each election season? And while the black community gets empty rhetoric that for over fifty years has produced little in the way of tangible results—positive results anyway—the Democrats gain the position and power to continue the destruction of the black community while we lose our morality, our potential, and the lives of millions of our unborn.

Just as Jesse Jackson has argued that one can't be black and oppose Obamacare, so Senate Majority Leader Harry Reid contended that one couldn't be Hispanic and support a Republican.[26] The Democrats' message to minorities, especially the black community, is that we are not smart enough to think for ourselves. The Democrats have asked us, most recently Michelle Obama, to let them do the thinking for us and we have obliged them. Like the high school teacher who controlled an entire class' behavior with candy, the Democrats have long controlled the black community's behavior with a single word: *racism*.

REVERSE RACISM

"Beloved, do not believe every spirit, but test the spirits, whether they are of God; because many false prophets have gone out into the world" (1 John 4:1).

While the Democrats and their surrogates—the national leadership of the NAACP, Jesse Jackson, Al Sharpton, and the Congressional Black Caucus—are always out scrounging around for instances of racism, they choose to ignore their own blatant acts of racism.

While Harry Reid and Democrats like to wrongly take credit for the passage of landmark civil rights legislation for blacks, they ignore the fact that in 1964 it was the Democrat Party led by Al Gore Sr., William Fulbright, mentor of "the first black president" Bill Clinton, and the recently deceased Robert Byrd, former Grand Wizard of the KKK, who worked to deny blacks the civil rights we so rightly deserved.

When President Clinton abolished welfare programs that went primarily to lower-class blacks, there was not a peep made by either so-called black leaders or the Democrats. Had someone named Bush, or any Republican for that matter, abolished those programs we would still be hearing claims of racism and of attempts to take us back to the days of slavery. But since these "reforms" were enacted by a Democrat, it's perfectly fine. When President Jimmy Carter referred to Obama as a "black boy," there was no outcry from the media or from Democrats, those great defenders of blacks.

Had a Republican made the statements Clinton reportedly made about Obama being the type of person who would be carrying their bags, or getting them coffee (Green, 2012), the media and the professional racists would still be talking about it. However, since those statements were made by a Democrat, he gets a pass not only from the media and black leaders but also from the black community.

When those blacks who were not born into a political party, those who have chosen to exercise their God-given right of free thought, those who have put the cross of Christ far above the golden jackass of the Democrat Party, are the targets of racist comments, the Democrats, and sadly most of the black community, find it amusing but not racist. When the likes of Supreme Court Justice Clarence Thomas, Dr. Alan Keyes, and Secretary of State Condoleeza Rice are called *oreos*, *sell-outs*, *house niggers*, *Aunt Jemima* and *Uncle Tom* by Democrats and their supporters, there's no outcry from so-called black leaders or the black community.

When Senator Christopher Dodd praised former KKK member Senator Robert Byrd (both of whom were Democrats) as "a great senator for any moment," there was no condemnation or cries of racism. But when Republican Senator Trent Lott praised Republican Senator Strom Thurmond, who never was a member of the KKK, and who after becoming a Republican defended blacks against lynching and discriminatory practices, Democrats and their attack dogs in the liberal media went crazy with claims of racism.[27]

When the most-racial president and his Attorney General Eric Holder dropped charges of voter intimidation against the New Black Panther Party after the case had already reportedly been won, the media and racism watchdogs were silent. According to FOX News (2009) the charges involve a 2008 election day incident at a Philadelphia voting center. The author contends that three members of the party, wearing paramilitary gear, with one brandishing a weapon, were accused of threatening voters. A civil suit filed in the waning days of the Bush administration accused the men of violating voters' rights by using coercion, threats and intimidation. The author posits that the Obama administration won the case in April, then went on to dismiss the charges in May.

The defendants (who of course never got the opportunity to be defendants, thanks to the most-racial president and Eric Holder's Department of Justice) were caught on tape brandishing weapons and making intimidating statements to white voters in a Philadelphia voting precinct.[28] Also, in a *WorldNet Daily* report, an Obama appointee, Deputy Assistant Attorney General Julie Fernandez, stated that "the voting section will not bring any other cases against blacks and other minorities."[29]

The Democrats and their surrogates are experts at finding racial discrimination under every stone and behind every door. In a bizarre twist of irony, however, they have exempted themselves from being considered racists, when in truth they are the biggest racists of all. As for the professional race-baiters in the black leadership, they have learned well from their Democrat masters. When they want to solicit donations, they go out and invent instances of racism. They've found racism in *Star Wars* characters, they've found racism in greeting cards, and now one liberal has found racism in the heartwarming story *The Blind Side,* the true story of a homeless young black male who was taken in by a white family and would later go on to play in the NFL. Incredibly someone has called the publicizing of this true story an act of racism. Why? Because the loving family that took this homeless young black man in was white.[30]

A similar charge of racism was leveled against philanthropist Robert Thompson when he offered to donate $200 million to fund fifteen new charter schools for the express purpose of giving parents in Detroit the option of getting their children out of under-performing schools. A *National Review Online* article stated that 70 percent of children and 47 percent of adults in Detroit are illiterate. When former Detroit Pistons star Dave Bing partnered with Thompson in an attempt to improve the education of young blacks, he was harshly criticized by "black leaders" and awarded a "Sambo Sell-Out Award."[31]

This is but one example of how our leaders continue to rob our young of a decent education. Thus, during an impressionable twelve-year period of their lives our young are surrendered to those on the left to be molded like clay. Children created by God are delivered to those who, by their own admission, believe they are the descendants of monkeys and single-celled organisms that crawled out of a puddle of primordial slime. And what a sad commentary on the black community when those who are fighting for a quality education for blacks are called racists. The professional racist is one who profits from keeping the races divided; he will invent racism where there is none.

THE RACIST REPUBLICANS

"They have also surrounded me with words of hatred, and
fought against me without a cause.
In return for my love they are my accusers,
But I give myself to prayer. Thus they have rewarded me evil for
good, And hatred for my love. Set a wicked man over him, and
let an accuser stand at his right hand" (Psalm 109:3–6).

From time to time I'll hear some black leader or political pundit proclaim that Republicans need to do more to reach out to blacks. Former congressman J. C. Watts made this claim during BHO's campaign for the presidency. None has ever explained exactly what "reaching out to the black community" means. But perhaps the Republicans would get more of the black vote if they followed the lead of the Democrat Party. Republicans could start by joining the Democrats in their constant attempts to totally outlaw Christ. They could join the Democrats in their attempts to turn America into a modern-day version of Sodom and Gomorrah. And if they really wanted to gain the black vote they could fight to increase the murders of unborn black children instead of trying to restrict or end them. Perhaps they could somehow find a way to codify into law that blacks are to receive only a substandard education. These are the things that the Democrats are doing to "reach out to the black community."

But, no, instead of fighting to increase the murder of unborn blacks, these terrible "racist" Republicans are constantly trying to restrict the practice and insist that all human life is sacred because it is created in the very image of God. Recently, these racists included a ban on the legalized murder of unborn babies in the continuing resolution bill to fund the government. Our friends in the Democrat Party, on the other hand, made it known that they would prefer not to pay members of the military or even shut down the entire government rather than oppose the taxpayer-funded murder of unborn babies.[32]

Perhaps if the Republicans of the past had opposed civil rights as the Democrats did, instead of fighting for them, blacks would find the party more appealing. Because then, as now, the Democrat Party knows what's best for blacks. Perhaps these racist Republicans could take a page from the past history of the Democrats and found a group similar to the Democrats' KKK. Or perhaps they should seek advice from the group that has murdered more blacks than the KKK, the Democrats' main ally, Margaret Sanger's Planned Parenthood.[33]

No. These so-called racist Republicans instead continue to push blacks away by contending for Christians' freedom of religion. They offend blacks by claiming that the God-ordained institution of marriage should be exclusively between one man and one woman. And they insult the dignity of blacks by claiming that the unborn have the same right to life as you, I, turtles, eagles, or dogs. These silly Republicans think that blacks should be able to remove their children from violent and under-performing schools and enroll them in schools that will give them a quality education. From their very beginnings when they were formed to put an end to slavery, to the forming of the Radical Republicans who considered Frederick Douglass one of their members, these racist Republicans have fought for the rights of blacks.[34] Sadly, no matter what history proves, and regardless of the reality before our eyes, the black community continues to hate the Republican Party.

As Middle Eastern terrorists were sending their young into Israel to blow themselves up, Israeli Prime Minister Golda Meir commented that the Palestinians hated Israel more than they loved their own children. Likewise, the black community's support for candidates and policies that attempt to outlaw our faith, demand the murder of our unborn, and promote the perverting of our young suggests that the black community also hates the Republican Party more than we love our own children.

Unfortunately, recent incarnations of the Republican leadership have begun to take their constituents for granted. Secure, I suspect, in their belief that conservatives and Christians have no choice but to support them no matter how they behave, they have produced empty rhetoric for the past few years and very little in the way of concrete results. Say what you will about those on the left, but they do get results. The do-nothing Republicans, however, seem content only to get elected. In 2010 and 2014, Republican supporters fought for and gained Republican majorities. For our efforts we have gotten rhetoric, excuses and theater, nice-sounding speeches about what they believe, excuses as to why they couldn't oppose BHO's liberal policies, and meaningless votes that produced no results. In recent years, the Republican leadership has been much like the scribes spoken of in Luke 20:46–47, *"Beware of the scribes, who desire to go around in long robes, love greetings in the marketplaces, the best seats in the synagogues, and the best places at feasts, who devour widows' houses, and for a pretense make long prayers. These will receive greater condemnation."* They promise results, but in the end they support the policies of those on the left. And yet, they are surprised at the support received by outsiders such as presidential candidates Donald Trump and Ben Carson, another indication of how out of touch the Republican establishment is with those who have supported them. Members of a recent focus group felt that businessman Donald Trump had the country's best interest at heart, while the Republican Party was only looking out for itself.[35]

When Paul Ryan became the new house speaker, conservatives expected that he would stand up for the conservative principles of the party. Instead, we got more of the same as we had gotten from Boehner: unconditional surrender and bitter betrayal. Republican congressional leaders, once again, ignored the concerns of those that voted them into power and behaved like magical genies, granting every wish of BHO and those on the left. Ryan and the spineless Republicans agreed to fund the child murderers of Planned Parenthood, to continue to protect foreign criminals in sanctuary cities, to fund BHO's climate-change agenda, to fund the settlement of foreign refugees, and to import even more foreign workers.[36]

Sadly, this Republican majority seems little different from a Democratic majority. When Donald Trump called for halting the import of Syrian refugees to America until we could be sure that they are not ISIS plants, Paul Ryan and Reince Priebus, doing their best impressions of BHO, ran to the defense of the potential terrorists. Displaying that they value the safety of Americans just as much as BHO, which is not at all, they joined the chorus of those on the left in condemning Mr. Trump's common-sense suggestion. Reid, I mean Ryan (it's hard to tell them apart), declared, "This is not conservatism. What was proposed [by Trump] is not what this party stands for. And more importantly, it's not what this country stands for."[37] I find myself agreeing totally with Ryan. It is not what this party stands for. Lately, it seems that this party has stood for nothing. Their spineless and weak leadership seems to only exist to betray those that put them in power and bow to the wishes of BHO and those on the left.

CHAPTER 2

THE COVENANT WITH DEATH

"Because you have said, 'We have made a covenant with death, and with Sheol we are in agreement. When the overflowing scourge passes through, it will not come to us, For we have made lies our refuge, and under falsehood we have hidden ourselves'" (Isaiah 28:15).

SACRIFICED THEIR
SONS AND DAUGHTERS

*"Yea, they sacrificed their sons and their daughters unto devils,
and shed innocent blood, even the blood of their sons and of
their daughters, whom they sacrificed unto the idols of Caanan:
and the land was polluted with blood"*
(Psalm 106:37–38).

What if there was an organization allied with the Republican Party, an organization created specifically for the extermination of the black race, an organization that set up slaughter factories in black neighborhoods? An organization that the Republican Party insisted must receive over $500 million taxpayer dollars yearly to carry out their murderous goals. An organization that had reduced the black community to a product, rather than to a people. If there were such an organization allied with the Republican Party, our black leaders and our churches would be out in full force against them. They would organize marches, hold press conferences, air TV ads, and take every available opportunity to expose such an evil and murderous organization.

Sadly, there is such an organization only it is allied with the Democrat Party, not the Republican Party. But you'll not find the so-called leaders of the black community or the pastors of black churches making any attempts to expose their systematic attack on the black community. Why? Because the great enabler of this murderous organization is the Democrat Party. Sadly, for many, especially so-called black leaders, the Democrat Party has taken the place of the God of creation in their hearts. While many of these leaders boldly claim to love and serve Christ, their actions expose who it is that they really serve. And they confirm Isaiah 29:13: *"Wherefore the Lord said, for as much as this people draw near me with their mouth, and with their lips do honour me, but their heart is far from me, and their fear toward me is taught by the precept of men."* They have cast aside the commandments of God and become accomplices of those on the left whose agenda is to totally outlaw Christ, promote the lifestyle of Sodom and Gomorrah, and even murder the nation's unborn children.

These "progressive" leaders, with the unquestioning support of, sadly, over 90 percent of the black community, are responsible for the slaughter of millions and millions of innocent babies. Since 1973, when the Supreme Court committed an atrocious case of judicial activism in the landmark abortion case *Roe v. Wade,* some 50 million innocent babies have been burned alive in a salty saline solution, sliced and diced into tiny pieces by scalpels originally intended to save lives, twisted and pulled limb from limb by the murderous instruments of death. They have had poison injected into their hearts and been stabbed in the backs of their skulls and had their brains suctioned out by high-powered vacuums.[1]

Someone once stated that the most dangerous place for a child in modern America is the womb. We live in a society that encourages, justifies, and defends the murder of unborn children and, sadly, many of those in the pro-life movement are not even willing to call it what it is: murder. Instead we have let those on the left redefine murder (the intentional taking of a human life) as "abortion" or other politically correct euphemism such as "pregnancy termination" or "the exercise of reproductive rights."

In Scripture, Jesus Himself tells us that there is no greater love than that one would give his life for a friend. *"Greater love has no one than this, than to lay down one's life for his friends"* (John 15:13). There is also no greater love than the sacrificing of one's children for the benefit of another, *"For God so loved the world that He gave His only begotten Son, that whoever believes in Him should not perish but have everlasting life"* (John 3:16).

We in the black community say that we are against the murder of unborn children, yet, out of a love for the Democrats, we have sacrificed the lives of millions and millions of our unborn sons and daughters. Consider this statement by National Organization of Women President Terry O'Neill, "Abortion, like contraception, is essential health care that saves lives."[2]

Those on the left continue to equate the miracle of pregnancy with the deadliest of diseases. They make it seem that every pregnant female is at a high risk for death. How incredibly ridiculous is such a statement that suggests that the best way to save lives is to murder innocent unborn babies. I'm accustomed to hearing those who advocate for child murder claim that it saves the lives of women. However, this ridiculous statement suggests that babies' lives can be saved by murdering them before they're even born. However, do not be deceived. Those in the business of murdering innocent babies are not concerned with the welfare of pregnant females, they are concerned with financial gain, nothing more, nothing less. There is little distinction between them and mass murderer Kermit Gosnell. I absolutely love the headline used by Matt Yonke in his LifeNews. com article: **"NOW President: Babies Wouldn't Die So Much if We'd Just Kill Them Before They Died!"[3]**

MARGARET SANGER

*"Also their bows will dash the young men to pieces, and they
will have no pity on the fruit of the womb; Their eye will not
spare children"
(Isaiah 13:18).*

The organization founded for the express purpose of eliminating the black race continues to thrive in our day. Margaret Sanger's Planned Parenthood is a major ally of the Democrat Party. Before Adolf Hitler there was Margaret Sanger. Sanger's plans for blacks, genocidal extermination, was the same as Hitler's plans for the Jewish people. Whereas Hitler sought the immediate extermination of Jews, Sanger, as subtle as the serpent, plotted to rid the country of blacks over a period of time. And whereas Hitler employed the German people in his scheme to eliminate Jews, Sanger's brilliant, but sinister, plan used influential blacks and the black church to help her pursue her goals of extermination of the black race. This was a stroke of evil genius.

Recognizing that blacks were a religious people, Sanger set out to use black pastors in her scheme. In 1939 she wrote, "hire three or more colored ministers, preferably with social service backgrounds, and with engaging personalities . . ." Why? Because she believed that "the most successful approach to the Negro is through a religious appeal. "We do not want word to get out that we want to exterminate the Negro population, and the minister is the man who can straighten out that idea if it ever occurs to any of their more rebellious members.""" [4]

Today, the likes of Barack Obama, Al Sharpton, Jesse Jackson, the NAACP, and the Congressional Black Caucus are playing the roles that Sanger defined for them to perfection. In her book *Pivot of Civilization*, Sanger wrote that, "colored people are like human weeds and are to be exterminated." She referred to blacks and other minorities as "reckless breeders, spawning human beings who never should have been born." And so, unwittingly aided by the well-meaning blacks of that period, Sanger set out to make sure that blacks were not born.

But unlike Hitler, who made no secret of his desire to exterminate the Jews, Sanger was deceptive in her plans. Like the modern Democrat Party and so-called black leaders, who for their own thirty pieces of silver have sold out their own, Sanger pretended to have the best interests of blacks at heart. There is even a Margaret Sanger Award that those who promote the murder of unborn children bestow upon that person who most zealously fights to promote the practice. In recent years, Hillary Clinton proudly accepted that dishonor.[41] Under the influence of those on the left, politicians, who once kissed babies while campaigning, are now rewarded for promoting the killing of babies as Planned Parenthood workers and Political Action Committees (PACs) have donated $25 million to Democrat candidates since 2000 (Paxton, 2015).

It is incredible that in today's information age any political party or organization could be so effective in getting a group of people to so completely participate in and vigorously defend grounds for their own destruction. But such is the case with the black community and the Democrat Party and their extermination wing, Planned Parenthood, and the entire child murdering industry.

The very fact that the Democrat Party and those in the business of murdering unborn children have been so effective in getting the black community to sacrifice their children to a political party brings to mind Ecclesiastes 1:9, *"That which has been is what will be, that which is done is what will be done, and there is nothing new under the sun."*

Just as Margaret Sanger persuaded the black leaders and churches of her time to promote the extermination of blacks, so the Democrat Party and Margaret Sanger's Planned Parenthood have enlisted today's black leaders and pastors in continuing her dream. And, sadly, because we as a people have placed political affiliation far ahead of the God whom most of us claim we serve, we, the black community, share in the complicity of those individuals who murder over one million innocent babies every year. For instance, in 2001, 2002, and 2003, then Senator Barack Hussein Obama single-handedly prevented the passage of an Illinois measure—the Born Alive Infant Protection Act—that would guarantee medical care for babies who survived the murderous attempt (ie, induced abortion).[5] Thus, it matters little to the Democrats whether the babies are unborn or newly born—all that matters is that they are exterminated. This is not "abortion," it is infanticide.

THE DEMOCRATS' COVENANT WITH DEATH

"Because you have said, "We have made a covenant with death, and with Sheol we are in agreement. When the overflowing scourge passes through, it will not come to us, For we have made lies our refuge, and under falsehood we have hidden ourselves""
(Isaiah 28:15).

Every attempt by those "racist Republicans" to end or limit the murder of unborn babies has met with resistance from the Democrat Party, black leaders, and the black community. This unwavering support has come even though Planned Parenthood has been caught red-handed on more than one occasion committing and supporting criminal activities.

In California, Victor Gonzalez, a former chief financial officer for Planned Parenthood of Los Angeles, filed a lawsuit after being fired for voicing his concerns over Planned Parenthood's illegal accounting practices. According to Gonzalez, the organization has been using fraudulent billing practices to overcharge California's Department of Health Services since at least 1997. Some estimate that Planned Parenthood may have defrauded the state of California out of more than $180 million taxpayer dollars.[7]

This time none other than Governor Arnold Schwarzenegger, a prime example of the Republican leadership's habit of promoting politics over principle (Governor Schwarzenegger has done for California what President Obama has done for America. He has taken a terrible situation and made it exponentially worse), came to Planned Parenthood's rescue. The Republican establishment's Schwarzenegger signed into law a bill that made the criminal activities of Planned Parenthood legal.

In Birmingham, Alabama, a Planned Parenthood worker was caught on tape attempting to help a client whom she thought was a 14-year-old girl circumvent the state's parental notification law in order to illegally murder her unborn child. The Planned Parenthood worker also promised to help cover up statutory rape when she learned that the 14-year-old girl's boyfriend was a 31-year-old man. In Alabama, intercourse between a 14-year-old child and a 31-year-old adult is a felony.

In both Oklahoma and New Mexico, further proof that Margaret Sanger's dreams of exterminating the black race live on, Planned Parenthood employees were caught on video agreeing to use donations specifically for the purpose of murdering unborn black babies (Baggot, 2008). Planned Parenthood of Kansas and Mid-Missouri is facing a 107-count criminal complaint investigating document forgery and the illegal murder of post-viable babies.[8]

As I write this, after yet more video evidence showing Planned Parenthood workers in three states and the District of Columbia attempting to assist sex traffickers and arrange to illegally murder the babies of under-aged victims of sex trafficking, the US House of Representatives, controlled by a "racist Republican" majority, has voted to defund Margaret Sanger's Planned Parenthood. Black Attorney General Eric Holder, however, has indicated that the Department of Justice would not be prosecuting any of those caught on video attempting to assist what they thought was a sex-trafficking operation. In fact, if the Obama administration stays true to form they will probably find some way to prosecute the undercover investigators and give the child murderers at Planned Parenthood another raise.[9] Despite all of these violations, despite videotaped evidence of this behavior, and despite recent videotaped evidence that exposed Planned Parenthood's practice of selling baby body parts, the Obama administration continues to support the group. So loyal is the president to the Democrats' covenant with Planned Parenthood that he has informed those states that defunded the organization, in light of the selling of baby body parts revelation, that it is illegal to defund the group (Ertelt, 2016).

In light of Planned Parenthood's illegal activities, House Republicans (those vile, terrible racists), have attempted to strip the organization of the more than $1 million a day of taxpayer funds that they receive. As the House and Senate debated a continuing resolution that would fund the government until the end of 2011, Democrats declared that any attempts to defund Planned Parenthood in light of their many acts of criminal behavior (such as the amendment proposed by Indiana's Mike Pence) would be rejected. It mattered not to those on the left, Democrats, that Margaret Sanger's Planned Parenthood had provided cover for the rapists of underage girls, provided aid to sex traffickers who victimize underage girls, and demonstrated a willingness to accept donations for the express purpose of murdering unborn black babies.

Senate Majority Leader Harry Reid has vowed that the Democrats would see the government shut down before they would deny Planned Parenthood any taxpayer dollars. In a move that should expose what the Democrats truly value, the party has shown a willingness to cut military funding rather than to deny taxpayer dollars to the child murderers at Planned Parenthood. *"For where your treasure is, there your heart will be also"* (Matt. 6:21). Their hearts are surely with those who profit from the legalized murder of unborn children.

Today, Republicans express shock and outrage because of the videos that exposed Margaret Sanger's Planned Parenthood's habit of selling the parts of murdered unborn babies. But, this revelation is not breaking news. It was the suspicion of Planned Parenthood selling the parts of the unborn that they murdered for profit that led to a 2000 law passed in Kansas that covered the "harvesting" of the body parts of the murdered unborn.[10] Those who oppose the murder of unborn children are constantly told that such actions are personal and private. Why then are tax payers forced to participate in these child murders by surrendering approximately $500 million yearly to a murderous organization that boasts over 90 percent of its "services" as abortions.[11] With mounting calls for investigations and the defunding of Planned Parenthood, Democrats have vowed to defend and preserve their covenant with death. " *Because you have said, "We have made a covenant with death, and with Sheol we are in agreement. When the overflowing scourge passes through, it will not come to us, for we have made lies our refuge, and under falsehood we have hidden ourselves"* (Isa. 28:15). Instead of investigating Planned Parenthood, a number of Democrats including Nancy Pelosi, Jan Schakowsky, Zoe Lofgren, Jerrold Nadler, and Yvette Clarke suggest investigating the group who exposed Planned Parenthood's demonic deeds.[12] Hillary Clinton, while calling the images from the video "disturbing," was quick to defend Planned Parenthood, pointing to the years of good work that they have supposedly done, and like the others who defend child murders and barbarism, insinuating that perhaps those who exposed Planned Parenthood's demonic practices should be investigated.[13, 14] Pennsylvania's so-called "pro-life" senator, Bob Casey, the personification of a lie, has declared that he will oppose any efforts to defund Planned Parenthood (Gallagher, 2015).[15] Harry Reid, perhaps emboldened by the Republicans' past failures to defund Planned Parenthood quipped, "Good luck with that." Democratic Senator Patty Murray came to Planned Parenthood's defense by characterizing the murder of the unborn as healthcare for women.[16] *"Also their bows will dash the young men to pieces, and they will have no pity on the fruit of the womb; Their eye will not spare children"* (Isa. 13:18).

And this is their covenant with death. The Democrats will continue to ensure that Margaret Sanger's Planned Parenthood continues to receive over $1 million of taxpayer funds per day, regardless of any unlawful behavior they promote, and in turn Planned Parenthood will, during election seasons, use a portion of those funds to support Democrat candidates (Paxton, 2015). " *Getting treasures by a lying tongue Is the fleeting fantasy of those who seek death*" (Prov. 21:6).

ABORTION'S EFFECTS
ON THE BLACK COMMUNITY

"By covetousness they will exploit you with deceptive words;
for a long time their judgment has not been idle, and their
destruction does¹ not slumber"
(2 Peter 2:3).

A nd while our so-called leaders continue to prosper in their service to those on the left, the black community continues to decline. Under their leadership, the black community has declined in moral standards, wisdom, and numbers. While black leaders continue to collect their thirty pieces of silver to follow Margaret Sanger's plan to the letter, the black community suffers the horrible effects of the legalized murder of the unborn (abortion).

According to data from the CDC, the murder of the unborn (abortion) accounts for the deaths of more black Americans than the seven leading causes of death combined. In 2005, the state-sanctioned murder of unborn babies (abortion) was the killer of at least 203,991 black babies in the 36 states and 2 cities that kept data on the number of unborn babies murdered according to race. During the same period 198,385 blacks in all of America died from the seven leading causes of death for black Americans in 2005: heart disease, cancer, stroke, accidents, diabetes, homicide, and chronic lower respiratory diseases.[17]

It is quite possible that the number of black babies murdered before birth has increased since 2005. Since Obama was elected, he has attempted to provide taxpayer funds to murder unborn black babies in Washington, DC, while also eliminating the program that allowed black parents to get their children out of unproductive violent schools. His administration has been an advocate for beginning the practice of murdering unborn babies on military bases.

A mailing from Father Frank Pavone of Priests for Life reveals even more disturbing information from a report by Gospel of Life Ministries, dated December 14, 2009:

- The number of black babies murdered before birth is almost equal to the number that are actually born.

- Black females are almost five times as likely to have their child murdered before birth than white females are.

- While blacks comprise only 13 percent of the population, they provide 36 percent of the business for those in the business of state-sanctioned child murder (abortion).

- Since 1973 the state-sanctioned murder of unborn babies has been the cause of death for over 25 percent of black Americans.

- In the last thirty years the murder of the unborn (abortion) has been the cause of death for more than twice as many blacks as AIDS, accidents, violent crimes, cancer, and heart disease combined.

- Every four days the murder of unborn babies claims the lives of more blacks than the KKK lynchings claimed over a 150-year period.

One of the crown jewels of the Democrat Party, Planned Parenthood, operates the largest chain of state-sanctioned child murdering houses in America and an estimated 78 percent of their slaughter houses are strategically placed in black and minority communities.

As well as continuing Margaret Sanger's goal of exterminating the Negro race, state-sanctioned murder of unborn black babies is also very profitable. Those in the business of legally murdering unborn black babies collect more than $16,000 every hour, every day, 24 hours a day.

Aside from decimating the black community, the murder of unborn babies has also had a negative effect on the entire nation. While career politicians posture and pretend to be concerned about the bankrupting of Social Security, they continue to ignore one of the reasons the nation finds itself with the problem. Namely, that millions of citizens who would have been paying into the Social Security system were never afforded the opportunity to be born. Politicians will put the blame on Americans living longer and on Baby Boomers becoming eligible for SSI and totally ignore the estimated 45 million citizens (according to the most conservative figure; some estimate the number is actually 60 million) murdered before they ever drew breath who would have been paying into the system. And if we assume that some of these 45 million had children the number would be exponentially greater.

And it is this murder of unborn babies that is of the utmost importance to the Democrat Party. In fact, it is far more important than funding the government and certainly more important than funding the brave men and women who are defending our country against terrorists and tyrants. And another so-called "friend" of the black community, US Supreme Court Justice Ruth Bader Ginsburg, recently confirmed that the purpose of state-sanctioned murder of the unborn (abortion) is to get rid of the undesirable people. Margaret Sanger, of course, made it clear just who those undesirables are—the black community. In an interview conducted by Emily Bazelon of the *New York Times*, liberal Supreme Court Justice Ruth Bader Ginsburg revealed that she expected *Roe v. Wade* to take care of the concern of over-population growth and particularly the increase of those people of whom we do not want too many. Ginsburg's use of the word *we* in her actual statement speaks volumes and indicates that those on the left, liberals and Democrats, are still actively pursuing Sanger's goals. Had a conservative made such a statement, it would have been a major news story. But, since Ginsburg is a liberal, a woman of the left, it was completely ignored by what passes as the media today.

Democrats and black leaders . . . where would the black community be without them? They could instruct the colonial slave masters on how to effectively exploit a people. Through their promotion of the legalized murder of the unborn, they have turned unborn babies into a cash crop for themselves and Margaret Sanger's Planned Parenthood.

CHAPTER 3

BLACK LEADERSHIP

"'For among My people are found wicked men; They lie in wait as one who sets snares; They set a trap; They catch men. As a cage is full of birds, so their houses are full of deceit. Therefore they have become great and grown rich" (Jer. 5:26–27).

BLACK LEADERS

*"Everyone will deceive his neighbor, and will not speak the
truth; they have taught their tongue to speak lies; they weary
themselves to commit iniquity. Your dwelling place is in the
midst of deceit; Through deceit they refuse to know Me,"
says the Lord"
(Jer. 9:5–6).*

In 1903, W. E. B. Du Bois dreamed of an America in which
those few professionally educated blacks would return to their
communities and use their skills to benefit the members of those
communities. He called this group that would elevate us all "the
talented tenth."[1] Sadly, the talented tenth in America has done
exactly the opposite of what Mr. Du Bois envisioned. Instead
of elevating us they have pulled us down; instead of helping us,
they have harmed us. Possessing all of this world's goods, they
encourage the common man to support those whose policies have
greatly limited the potential of the black community. They are
actors, singers, producers, legislators, and even some pastors. With
yearly salaries that far exceed what many blacks can expect to earn
in a lifetime, they encourage many of the things which harm the
black community, such as liberal policies and hostility toward law
enforcement. And yet, they are silent on issues such as the high
unemployment rate of blacks, the state of the black family, and
the sub-standard education that blacks and minorities receive when
compared to whites.

Given that the policies of the Democrat Party are decimating the black community, one must wonder where those black leaders we frequently hear about are—the likes of Jesse Jackson, Al Sharpton, John Lewis, the NAACP, and the Congressional Black Caucus. While I am loath to even call these individuals and groups leaders, the truth is that they *are* leaders. And where they have been leading us is to our detriment. They have allied themselves with those on the left and convinced an entire race of people to consistently vote in favor of the very things we say we are against—hostility towards Christians, the murder of the unborn, the lifestyle of Sodom and Gomorrah, and opposition to school choice—and against the things the very things we say we support—faith in Christ, life, morality, and a better future and education for our children. The very sad truth is that these so-called "black leaders" are the major source of the black community's problems. In exchange for their own thirty pieces of silver, these "leaders" have sold the future and the lives of our people to the Democrat Party and those on the left.

Just as the Romans used the religious leaders of Jesus' time to help exert control over the Jewish people, so those on the left and the Democrats in our day use these black leaders to control and manipulate the black community. Without the willing aid of these "black leaders," those on the left could never exercise such total control over the lives and very thoughts of blacks. They pretend to care about the black community while ignoring our most significant problems.

> *But these, like natural brute beasts made to be caught and destroyed, speak evil of the things they do not understand, and will utterly perish in their own corruption, and will receive the wages of unrighteousness, as those who count it pleasure to carouse in the daytime. They are spots and blemishes, carousing in their own deceptions while they feast with you, having eyes full of adultery and that cannot cease from sin, enticing unstable souls. They have a heart trained in covetous practices, and are*

accursed children. They have forsaken the right way and gone astray, following the way of Balaam the son of Beor, who loved the wages of unrighteousness (2 Peter 2:12–15).

Those significant problems are directly or indirectly related to the policies of the Democrat Party, such as the murder of the unborn, out of wedlock births, the promotion of perversion among our young, substandard educational opportunities, and a separation from the God of creation through attempts to outlaw Christ and the free exercise of worship. Ironically, you won't find any of our leaders addressing these problems. Instead, they address issues that we have been taught to believe are the results of a concerted plot by the Republicans to keep us down. They address issues designed to mobilize us to get out and vote for the party that is determined to keep us as social slaves through their destructive programs or to destroy us by murdering our unborn and exterminating our race per Margaret Sanger's explicit plot to rid the world of Negroes.

For example, a mailing from the National Urban League cites these statistics:

1   Four decades after civil rights became the law of the land, black men and women earn less than 60 cents for each dollar white men earn in the private sector.
2   More than 1 in 5 black homeowners is facing foreclosure.
3   In a time when 1 in 8 Americans relies on food stamps to ward off hunger—a horrifying fact in its own right—1 black child of every 3 is growing up in poverty.
4   Black unemployment hovers near 16 percent, a figure much higher than the national average of 9 percent.

Missing from the National Urban League's list of challenges facing the black community are:

1   Approximately 1,500 unborn black babies are murdered each and every day. Surely murder is more horrifying than having to rely on food stamps for food. If you're denied life, of course, you have no need of food.

"Therefore I say to you, do not worry about your life, what you will eat or what you will drink; nor about your body, what you will put on. Is not life more than food and the body more than clothing?" (Matt. 6:25)

2   Minority students perform at or below the levels of 30 years ago (Zhao, 2012) and the gap between blacks and whites in math and reading scores has increased 5 points from 1992 to 2013 (Lee, 2014).

3   72 percent of black children are born out of wedlock.[2]

Al Sharpton's National Action Network recently protested the prosecution of Kelly Williams-Bolar, a single black mother, for using her father's address to send her daughters to a school where they would get a better education than the one they were forced to attend. While on the surface Sharpton's protest appears admirable, if one looks beneath the surface, he will find that it is a hollow and hypocritical show that ultimately benefits Sharpton and Sharpton alone.

He received positive press from the appearance of fighting for this courageous woman's right to seek the best education for her children and then returned to fighting to elect the very people whose policies have placed the mother in this unfortunate position. If the black community would only look beyond the empty rhetoric of black leaders, we would find that this type of traitorous deception is all too common in those individuals and groups whom those on the left have designated as black leaders.

With the aid of black leaders, the Democrat Party creates most of the problems facing the black community and then joins with them to blame the Republicans for those problems. And since the Republicans, for whatever reason, lack the backbone to defend themselves from the lies of the Democrats and their modern-day overseers, the so-called black leaders, the Democrats' version of the truth goes unchallenged.

After nearly fifty years of being more faithful to this political party than we have been to God, the black community has very little to show for it. As a people, we have gone backward, not forward. Our numbers have decreased because we have offered up our unborn children to the child murderers of the Democrat Party. Merely mentioning Jesus Christ's name can be a federal offense if done in public. Far from receiving a proper education, our young are being indoctrinated, not educated, to accept and embrace perversion while rejecting the founding principles of this nation and vilifying some of the great men of American history.

Instead of fighting for a proper education for our children, these so-called "leaders" prefer to lower the standards as if blacks were incapable of performing as well as members of other races. As a result, the Department of Justice, then led by the corrupt Eric Holder, forced the Dayton Police to lower the testing standards so that blacks might pass and qualify to become police officers. Thus, instead of demanding accountability from the educational system the Democrats and their servants in the black leadership prefer to keep black students trapped in failing schools and reward the school systems for failure. Failing schools are rewarded with more funds, and for failing students the standards are simply lowered. Even as it rails against the racism of American society and the nation's police departments, the Obama administration has approved the plans of twenty-six states to set lower academic achievement standards for minorities.[3] The implication of these types of standards seems to be that the Obama administration, and many of our nation's educators have decided that minorities are incapable of learning at the same level as whites, that we are intellectually inferior.

These new lowered standards will only lead to future instances of blacks being unable to pass employment exams such as the example from Ohio. And I expect that these lower requirements will also give our young the message that they are in fact intellectually inferior. This is the soft bigotry of low expectations that former President

George H. W. Bush spoke of. This is nothing short of another form of segregation. Just as BHO has given back the gains that our troops made in Iraq, he has given back the victory of *Brown v. the Board of Education*. This deliberate "dumbing down" of blacks renders us more manageable and is a calculated plan to keep us in a state of permanent servitude, willing to do the Democrats' bidding without critical thinking or asking questions.

This opinion of blacks as mindless drones, useful only to do the will of the Democrats, was recently displayed when Michelle Obama told blacks that we should always vote for Democrats. She stated that regardless of who was running or what they had done, we should always vote for Democrats and teach our children to vote for Democrats. She instructed blacks that we should not bother to think, just vote for Democrats. And then reward ourselves with some good old fried chicken.[4]

Furthermore, black leaders allied with the Democrat Party send the message that merely providing proof of one's ID at a polling place is a task far too difficult for blacks. We have bank accounts and credit cards, we own homes and pay our utility bills, we enroll in schools and colleges. All of these things and more require proof of one's ID. Yet black leaders, under the direction of those on the left, contend that providing proof that we're eligible to vote, as Americans, in American elections, is far beyond the capabilities of the average black person. Those with eyes to see and ears to hear will recognize what is behind this supposed *concern* for the voting rights of minorities and see it for what it is—an attempt to allow citizens of other countries to have a part in choosing America's leaders and an attempt to allow unscrupulous individuals to cast multiple votes to steal elections that cannot be won fairly.

While they claim to be concerned about the integrity of the vote, the Obama administration has resisted every effort by states to remove the dead from the voting rolls. And while those on the left, the Obama administration, black leaders, and liberal Democrats are fighting to allow those who are not American citizens to vote, they are fighting, and have fought, equally hard to exclude the votes of the brave men and women of the US military. While they claim to want every vote to count, on more than one occasion the Democrats have sought to use the courts to nullify the votes of those in the military.

For example, on July 17, 2012, the Obama for America Campaign, the Democratic National Convention, and the Ohio Democratic Party filed a suit to strike down part of an Ohio law that gives members of the military extra time to cast their ballots.[5]

This is not the first time the Democrat Party has attempted to "disenfranchise," as liberals like to say, the votes of those who put their lives on the line for our country. In 2000, then-presidential candidate Al Gore had his lawyers disqualify the ballots of soldiers serving overseas.[6] Is anything more devious than this—that a man who would be the leader of our troops, none other than the Commander-in-Chief, would fight to deny them the right to play a part in choosing that leader? And twelve years later the Obama administration attempted to resort to the same dirty tactics. And while they resort to the most underhanded of tactics, they continue to pay lip service to the cause of ensuring that black voters aren't discriminated against.

When I was a boy, we simply wanted fair and equal treatment. But the Democrats and their servants, black leadership, have convinced us that we are somehow due special treatment. They have convinced us to blame today's society for the actions of those in the past. Thanks to the Democrats the programs created to "even the playing field" for blacks have not had the intended effect. The trillions of dollars spent on the "war on poverty," welfare, food stamps, rent supplements, Section 8 housing, Pell Grants, and, probably more programs than I'm aware of, have been nullified by the attitude of entitlement and the victim mentality that the Democrats, aided by black leaders and some churches, have fostered among the black community.

The sad fact is that those we blindly support have little interest in seeing us receive anything that even remotely resembles a quality education. To them we are nothing more than a product to be used during election season for our votes and then cast aside. Our unborn children have become a cash crop for them and their allies in the child murdering industry. And still, remarkably, we continue to support and defend them.

BLACK LEADERS AND PLANNED PARENTHOOD

"They even sacrificed their sons and their daughters to demons,
and shed innocent blood,
The blood of their sons and daughters, whom they sacrificed to
the idols of Canaan;
And the land was polluted with blood"
(Psalm 106:37–38).

Margaret Sanger was a racist without peer who started Planned Parenthood specifically for the purpose of exterminating blacks. She considered blacks to be defective morons who should never have been born. And so Margaret Sanger set out to murder blacks before their births. To assist her in her murderous task, she enlisted the aid of black pastors. Today Margaret Sanger's Planned Parenthood has the full cooperation of not only so-called "black leaders" but also the most influential black leader of all—the current resident of the White House.

The leadership of the NAACP, Jesse Jackson's Rainbow Coalition, the Urban League, and those in a position to most benefit the black community, the Congressional Black Caucus, have been accessories in the destruction of the black community. They have joined the Democrat Party in the same way that those black pastors joined Margaret Sanger in her attempt to exterminate the black race.

"My son, if sinners entice you, do not consent. If they say, "Come with us, Let us lie in wait to shed blood; Let us lurk secretly for the innocent without cause; Let us swallow them alive like Sheol, And whole, like those who go down to the Pit; We shall find all kinds of precious possessions, We shall fill our houses with spoil; Cast in your lot among us, Let us all have one purse" (Prov. 1:10–14).

Having no shame, the *Reverends* Je$$e Jackson and Al Sharpton brazenly promote the murder of innocent babies while pretending to be representatives of Christ.

"For such are false apostles, deceitful workers, transforming themselves into apostles of Christ. And no wonder! For Satan himself transforms himself into an angel of light. Therefore, it is no great thing if his ministers also transform themselves into ministers of righteousness, whose end will be according to their works" (2 Cor. 11:13–15).

They present themselves as men of God, honoring him with their lips, but their hearts are full of darkness and deceit.

"Righteous are You, O Lord, when I plead with You; yet let me talk with You about Your judgments. Why does the way of the wicked prosper? Why are those happy who deal so treacherously? You have planted them, yes, they have taken root; They grow, yes, they bear fruit. You are near in their mouth but far from their mind" (Jer. 12:1–2).

When there are pro-life marches and rallies, these black leaders are nowhere to be found. Shamelessly, with not one iota of proof, some black leaders will claim that the virus that causes AIDS was created in a lab for the specific purpose of killing blacks. Yet they turn a blind eye to the published words of Planned Parenthood's Margaret Sanger who admitted that she started promoting the murder of the unborn (abortion), with the help of black leaders, for the sole purpose of eliminating the black race. These traitors will scrounge the bottom of the barrel searching for racism in movies, animated characters, voter ID laws, and even greeting cards but they dare not oppose their liberal masters who are promoting the murder of unborn black babies.

NAACP

"Her princes in her midst are like wolves tearing the prey, to shed blood, to destroy people, and to get dishonest gain"
(Ezek. 22:27).

Consider the NAACP, a group founded with the noblest of purposes—for the *advancement* of blacks—which has become a tool of the Democrat Party. On the international stage, the American student ranks near the bottom when compared to other nations,[7] and in America, black students rank at the bottom in academic performance. Far too many of our students are functionally illiterate, meaning they cannot adequately read or write to perform well in the business and professional spheres. Those who can read and write are performing below their grade level.

According to Zhao (2012), black and Latino students are performing at the same levels of blacks from 30 years ago, meaning that in 2012 blacks were receiving a 1982 education. It is not, as some racists have suggested, that blacks are intellectually inferior to whites. Given the same educational opportunities, the average black student will perform on at least the same level as their white counterparts. But sadly, blacks have been denied the same opportunities. Historically, black students have been trapped in under-performing schools, and many schools in poor black neighborhoods simply don't have the resources to provide students with quality educational experiences.

In times past, the case could be rightfully made that racism denied blacks a proper education. But today we have the opposite case: It is blacks, by virtue of the Democrat legislators that we support, who are denying blacks a proper education. Liberals, along with black leaders, have condemned blacks to indoctrination, not education. And any attempt to change that will be met by stiff resistance, as seen in the case of previously mentioned philanthropist Robert Thompson and Dave Bing.

The Republicans, those racists, have attempted to give parents a choice in the schools their children attend. Through the use of vouchers, the Republicans and school choice advocates have sought to give blacks a way to escape under-performing and violent schools. But the NAACP, President Barack Obama, and other black leaders are against school choice for black students.

An NAACP flyer states: "The fundamental goal of the NAACP'S education advocacy agenda is to provide all students access to quality education." Yet in 2006 the NAACP spearheaded the efforts to deny blacks a chance at getting such a quality education. They joined those who have a vested interest in ensuring that blacks aren't properly educated, Democrat-led public school and teacher unions, to have a voucher program designed to give blacks and poor students a chance at a quality education in Florida deemed unconstitutional.[8] After he was elected, President Barack Obama ensured that a voucher program in Washington, DC, was also killed.[63] And I'm willing to bet that most of these black leaders who fight so hard to keep black students in violent and under-performing schools send their own children to private schools where they can get a quality education. In the meantime, they condemn our children to liberal school systems that, despite the obvious differences of the male and female anatomy, cannot even make the distinction between male and female. A saying attributed to an unnamed member of the KKK holds that "if you want to hide something from a black man, simply put it in a book." The actions of the Democrat Party, black leaders, and President Obama suggest that they agree with this saying, and they definitely seem to be trying to hide their actions and true motives from the black community. What actions and motives? The fact that they are part of a concerted effort that has sold the lives and potential of the entire black community to those on the left and that their motives are the same as the motives of Judas so long ago.

For years the NAACP claimed not to have an official position on the murder of the unborn while supporting those candidates who fought vigorously for it. Then in 2004 the NAACP came out with a resolution that voiced support for equal access to the legalized murder of unborn babies (abortion) and urged its members to participate in a rally encouraging the legalized murder of innocent unborn babies (abortion) in Washington, DC.[9] Then in 2007, when those NAACP members who recognized the murder of the unborn for what it was and for what it was doing to the black community, and the country proposed a resolution expressing opposition to the murder of the unborn, the NAACP blocked the resolution.[10] This was the second time in four years that the leadership of the NAACP had blocked such a resolution.

In Georgia, the NAACP has a history of first endorsing and then rescinding their endorsement of pro-life measures aimed at minimizing the murder of unborn black children. Most recently they endorsed a bill that would criminalize murdering a pre-born child because of his or her race (so-called "gender selection" abortion). Earlier, when Georgia Right to Life sought the NAACP's endorsement for the Prenatal Nondiscrimination Act, the NAACP initially gave it, only once again to rescind the endorsement. In both cases the leadership in the Georgia NAACP later claimed that they had not understood what they were endorsing.

And here is an example of how little the NAACP truly cares for the black community. A few years ago the President/CEO of the NAACP Kweisi Mfume, who himself had served five terms as a Democrat congressman from Maryland, protested the methods that KFC used to kill their chickens.[11] Al Sharpton also came to the defense of chickens destined for the fryer. Yet when it came to the horrific murder of millions of unborn babies (abortion), the NAACP (no longer pretending not to have a position) voiced their support for abortion and suppressed any dissenting voices. They have cast their full support behind Margaret Sanger's vision for the black community. They should drop all pretenses and change their name, as someone suggested, to the National Association for the Abortion of Colored People.

Their latest despicable acts on behalf of their masters is to run crying to the United Nations in an attempt to block the voter ID laws of several states.[12] This action, like all of the actions of the professional racists we call black leaders, has nothing to do with the fair and equal treatment of blacks but rather is designed to benefit their masters of the Democrat Party. With Obama's now largely discredited ACORN no longer able to commit voter fraud openly, the Democrats must now rely on the votes of those who are in the country *illegally* or are otherwise not legally entitled to vote. Thus we have the NAACP, who value the treatment of chickens destined for the fryer more than the quality of human life, and indeed the very lives of blacks, mobilizing to gain *illegal* votes for their slave masters.

The NAACP has been reduced to the role of attack dog that is let out at the first sign of any opposition to those on the left. The Democrat Party sends them out to attack any who would threaten their product—the black community. Like the boy who cried wolf, these leaders are constantly crying racism. They have been reduced to scrounging about for racism in movies and greeting cards and, during election seasons, in anyone who dares to simply disagree with a Democrat candidate or Democrat policies.

Finally, I must specify that it is the leadership of the NAACP that I'm laying these claims against. Here where I live it was the NAACP's Dorothy Scott that got satisfaction for my family when it appeared that the local school system was attempting to deny my special needs niece the opportunity to reach her full potential. Where my sister and mother seemed to be fighting an uphill battle,

Ms. Scott came along and ensured that my niece was afforded every opportunity to reach her full potential. Today, thanks in part to Ms. Scott, my niece is taking college courses. Sadly, there appear to be no Dorothy Scotts in the national leadership.

JE$$E JACKSON

They profess to know God, but in works they deny Him, being abominable, disobedient, and disqualified for every good work (Titus 1:16).

Then there is the *reverend* Je$$e Jackson. Adulterer, extortionist, traitor to his people, and advocate for the murder of millions of unborn babies, black and white. Mr. Jackson, in all his greatness, has taken it upon himself to decide who is and who is not a black man. As I mentioned earlier, during a reception hosted by the Congressional Black Culprits, er . . . Caucus, Je$$e Jack$on stated that "you can't vote against healthcare and call yourself a black man."[13] Mr. Jackson's insulting remarks were directed at one Arthur Davis, Democrat from Alabama, who made the mistake of exercising his free will. The Democrat Party strictly prohibits such exercise of free will on the part of a black person. To the Democrats, blacks today, like the slaves of the past, are the property of the Democrats, who will dictate how we think and how we act, and if they want our opinions they will give them to us.

The recent revelations by Obamacare architect, Jonathan Gruber, verifies what many in the Tea Party and other opponents of hell's care reform had been saying all along: that the bill would cause many to lose their current healthcare plans and be forced to fund and use an inferior product. Of all those in the Congressional Black Caucus, Mr. Davis was the only one who didn't realize that blacks remain the possession of the Democrat slave masters. Bravo to you, Mr. Arthur Davis!

Mr. Jackson's remarks, insulting to all blacks who exercise their God-given ability to think for themselves, did not rise to the level of racism that it would have if a Republican (black or white) had spoken them. To Mr. Jackson, Obama's healthcare reform, predicated on the murder of unborn innocents (abortion) is good and any opposition to it is evil. *"Woe to those who call evil good, and good evil; Who put darkness for light, and light for darkness; Who put bitter for sweet, and sweet for bitter."* (Isaiah 5:20).

Mr. Jackson presents himself to the world as a man of the cloth fighting for justice for his people. But his actions reveal the character of a criminal blackmailer and extortionist. *"Woe to you, scribes and Pharisees, hypocrites! For you cleanse the outside of the cup and dish, but inside they are full of extortion and self-indulgence"* (Matthew 23:25).

Jackson has made himself a lucrative living by feigning concern for the black community. Of the perhaps millions of dollars that he has extorted from corporations (by threatening boycotts and claims of racism if said companies do not comply with his demands), how much of it has actually benefited the black community? In the early 1980s, through an act of extortion and intimidation, this con artist secured an Anheuser-Busch distributorship for his sons.[14] After this grand payoff the Jackson initiated boycott against Anheuser-Busch products went away. And it is not just Anheuser Busch, many corporations have fallen victim to this chief extortionist—among which are Toyota, Citibank, Coca-Cola, NASCAR, General Electric, and many others—who have chosen to "pay off" the extortionist rather than be accused of racism.[15] Even as he engages in extortion and promotes the murders of millions of unborn babies, Mr. Jackson brazenly continues to present himself as a man of God.

AL SHARPTON

"But there were also false prophets among the people, even as there will be false teachers among you, who will secretly bring in destructive heresies, even denying the Lord who bought them, and bring on themselves swift destruction. And many will follow their destructive ways, because of whom the way of truth will be blasphemed"
(2 Peter 2:1–2).

A t a time when unemployment among blacks is at 16 percent, the *Reverend* Al Sharpton can be found fighting to increase the influx of *illegal* immigrants to America. It matters not to this black leader that there are few jobs to be found in the country, or that the black community is suffering the brunt of this job shortage. This *reverend* is interested in two things—the national spotlight and pleasing the social slave masters of the Democrat Party. Sharpton says he will challenge Arizona's immigration law in the courts and has even suggested that *illegals* resist America's laws.[16] And as is the norm for all of these black leaders the *reverend* Sharpton has sought to identify those who are violating America's laws with the fight of blacks for civil rights, the rights of our ancestors who were brought here against their will. *Illegal* immigrants made a conscious decision to break our laws and voluntarily come here, and are constantly demanding to be rewarded for doing so.

When it was discovered that Frank Lombard, a white homosexual instructor at Duke University, had a habit of drugging his 6-year-old adopted black son and sodomizing him, these leaders did not so much as utter a peep.[17] This brazen instructor even went online and offered the young child to other child molesters for their perverted pleasure. And still no cries of racism or demands for an investigation from these traitorous leaders.

In March 2006, however, when a promiscuous black female of questionable reputation, Crystal Mangum, who now stands convicted of murder, accused some white members of the Duke lacrosse team of rape, these leaders immediately came out demanding the heads of these innocent young men. Immediately these black leaders, led by the *Reverends* Sharpton and Jackson, set about to ruin these young men's reputations.[18]

It is hard to believe that one person would fall for the same deception twice, but recall that Al Sharpton has a history of this sort of blind rush to judgment. In 1987, Sharpton ran to the defense of Tawana Brawley, a fifteen-year-old black girl who falsely accused police officers and a prosecuting attorney of rape. The case was a hoax, and Sharpton lost a defamation suit for ruining reputations and slandering innocent men. So Sharpton played "race hustler" in the case of a lying teenager, Tawana Brawley, who falsely accused white men of rape, and Crystal Mangum, who falsely accused the Duke lacrosse team of rape. But when a respected Duke instructor, liberal and homosexual pedophile, was proven to have committed perverted, deviant sexual acts against a six-year-old black child, neither Sharpton nor any of the influential black leaders responded with the outrage that they exhibited when Brawley and now Mangum spouted their lies.

What accounts for this? Well, to bring any negative attention to the deplorable acts of one who practices the lifestyle of Sodom and Gomorrah would be to go against the wishes of those on the left. Rather than opposing the lifestyle that the word of God calls vile, unnatural, wicked, and abominable, this *reverend* supports it. In January 2006 this *reverend* hosted a meeting in Atlanta between black pastors and homosexual activists, those who promote the lifestyle of Sodom and Gomorrah.[19] The goal of the meeting was to get these black pastors to reject the clear teaching of the word of God— *"You shall not lie with a male as with a woman. It is an abomination"* (Lev. 18:22)—and to accept the contentions of the homosexual activists that their lifestyle is both natural and healthy. In effect, the intent was to condemn the judgments of the God of creation so that those who live contrary to it might feel justified. *"Would you indeed annul My judgment? Would you condemn Me that you may be justified"* (Job 40:8)?

Events such as these lead me to agree with Obama when he states that America is *no longer a Christian nation.* If all Scripture is given by inspiration of God— *"All Scripture is given by inspiration of God, and is profitable for doctrine, for reproof, for correction, for instruction in righteousness"* (2 Timothy 3:16)—and if Scripture was written to serve as an example to Christians— *"For whatever things were written before were written for our learning, that we through the patience and comfort of the Scriptures might have hope"* (Romans 15:4)—then what in the world are Christian pastors doing entertaining the notion of supporting the lifestyle of Sodom and Gomorrah? Preach against homosexual persecution and discrimination, yes, but to endorse what God has called sinful, no. For many of us, myself included, those with same sex attractions are friends and family members. They are not some alien species to be mistreated or persecuted. They are fellow human beings created in the image of God. Scripture is clear on what God thinks of homosexuality; however, it also gives us examples of how we are to treat our fellow man, even those with whom we disagree.

In Luke 9:52–56 Jesus rebuked James and John who wanted to call fire down on the Samaritans for refusing to receive Jesus. In Luke 15:28–31, the story of the prodigal son, the father rebukes the older brother who was angry because the father celebrated the return of the prodigal. And in Jonah 4:2–11 God rebuked Jonah who was angry because God forgave, and did not destroy, sinful Nineveh.

As Christians we should desire the salvation, not the destruction, of homosexuals. No Christian should celebrate or seek to justify tragedies such as the Orlando night club massacre.

We have the example of Lot on how we should react to that lifestyle: *"for that righteous man, dwelling among them, tormented his righteous soul from day to day by seeing and hearing their lawless deeds"* (2 Peter 2:8). When we are told not to speak in Jesus' name, we have the example of Peter and John: *"But Peter and John answered and said to them, "Whether it is right in the sight of God to listen to you more than to God, you judge"* (Acts 4:19).

When we are required to participate in the slaughter of children we have the example of the Hebrew midwives: *"Then the king of Egypt spoke to the Hebrew midwives, of whom the name of one was Shiphrah and the name of the other Puah; and he said, "When you do the duties of a midwife for the Hebrew women, and see them on the birthstools, if it is a son, then you shall kill him; but if it is a daughter, then she shall live." But the midwives feared God, and did not do as the king of Egypt commanded them, but saved the male children alive"* (Ex. 1:15–17). The mature Christian, and most especially pastors, should have no need of being instructed on how to respond to those issues on which the scriptures are crystal clear. When we blatantly ignore the clearly expressed word of God in favor of political affiliation or popular culture, we make ourselves no different from Adam and Eve who rejected the instructions of God in favor of the serpent's advice.

This *reverend* Al Sharpton has demonstrated that he is willing to stoop to any level to gain the national spotlight. He has been accused of leading a riot in New York that led to the deaths of citizens and the destruction of property.[20] So, in the eyes of some he will always be remembered as Reverend Riot. Today, he is much more influential but still lacks anything slightly resembling a conscience. He has brought the same type of incitement to Ferguson, Missouri. He is a prime example of George Bernard Shaw's quote, "We learn from history that we learn nothing from history." Whether it's Tawana Brawley or Crystal Mangum, Crown Heights, New York or Ferguson, Missouri, this shakedown artist is not concerned with true justice, the lives of innocents, or property destruction. He sees only opportunities to further exploit the black community for his thirty pieces of silver.

And it is a sad commentary on our society that a man with reverend Sharpton's checkered history is rewarded with radio and television programs and even lands the anchor post on MSNBC's 6 o'clock news show *PoliticsNation with Al Sharpton*.

BLACK LEGISLATORS

"What are you willing to give me if I deliver Him to you?" And
they counted out to him thirty pieces of silver (Matt. 26:15).

And then there's the Congressional Black Caucus (CBC), the group in a position to immediately confront some of the problems of the black community. The very existence of the CBC is a prime example of the type of segregation that the civil rights leaders fought against. As a group, the CBC is not as well- known as Jackson, Sharpton, or Obama. But, like all those whom the liberal media have crowned as "black leaders," this group has sold the entire black community to the Democrat Party for position and profit. They are a classic example of the foxes who have been entrusted with guarding the hen house. These self-serving leaders have opened the door of the black community to the child murderers of the abortion industry. *"Her princes in her midst are like wolves tearing the prey, to shed blood, to destroy people, and to get dishonest gain"* (Ezek. 22:27).

They have spat in the face of the God of creation and of the black community by equating the demands of homosexuals, those who revel in the acts that doomed Sodom and Gomorrah, with the struggles of blacks for civil rights—civil rights that the Democrats fought every inch of the way. Blacks did not choose their skin color, but homosexuals choose their sexual preferences. There is no such thing as "sexual orientation." The genitals that a person are born with determine his or her orientation. We insult the God of creation and call Him unjust when we claim that He would force someone to engage in activities that He has condemned so strongly.

The CBC has blatantly betrayed the black community and think that they are qualified to instruct the Creator on what constitutes a marriage. *"Shall the one who contends with the Almighty correct Him? He who rebukes God, let him answer it"* (Job 40:2). And like the other leaders who are leading the black community to a future of mediocrity and government dependence, the Congressional Black Culprits are also committed to keeping our young trapped in schools that teach only the agenda of those on the left.

Our so-called black leaders blatantly undermine the potential of the black community all while smiling in our faces. These tools of the Democrat Party have indeed received profit and position in exchange for keeping the black community mentally and socially enslaved to the Democrats, but they fail to realize that they will never be seen as equals among the true racists of the Democrat Party.

When the ethics committee launches investigations, they are usually targeted at blacks. For instance, Representatives Charlie Rangel, Maxine Waters, and Roland Burris have been the focus of some of the more publicized investigations of black politicians.[21] Knowing that the majority of blacks are opposed to equating the God-ordained institution of marriage with the lifestyle of Sodom and Gomorrah, the CBC have thrown their support behind forcing acceptance of that lifestyle on Americans.

With blacks bearing the brunt of unemployment in America, the CBC is supporting the legalization of millions and millions of low-wage, low-skilled illegal immigrants. As many blacks already feel like second-class citizens, Obama, the CBC, and the Democrats are getting ready to demote us a notch. With the legalization of millions of illegal immigrants, get ready for third-class citizenship, we may be there already. The National Urban League's annual report "The State of Black America" already finds that in America Hispanics are better off than blacks.[22] While the topic of black unemployment has found its way into many articles, an education, which is required by many employers, has been largely ignored. Also not mentioned are teen pregnancy rates, high school drop-out rates or rates of incarceration. In "Fact Sheet: Outcomes for Young, Black Men," a 2014 article by Tamika Thompson, she observes:

- Only 54 percent of blacks graduate from high school, as compared to 75 percent of whites and Asians

- Black male students in grades K–12 were approximately 2 ½ times more likely to be suspended from school in 2000 as white students.

- The average black twelfth-grader reads at the same level as eighth-grade white students.

- Twelfth-grade blacks scored much lower in reading than those of every other racial group.

- A mere 14 percent of blacks score at or above the proficient level.

- The majority of those in US prisons and jails are minorities, people with mental health problems, drug addictions, low levels of education, and histories of unemployment and underemployment.

It is common knowledge that an education, a *proper* education, greatly increases one's chances of employment and success. But, our leaders, allied with the Democrats, have blocked every proposal to get our young out of under-performing liberal schools where they are indoctrinated not educated.

And there you have them—the "black leadership." They have shamelessly sold the black community to liberal Democrats. Our young are trapped in under-performing schools and taught to embrace promiscuity and perversion. An estimated 13 million blacks delivered to Margaret Sanger's Planned Parenthood and others in the child-murdering industry. The religious leaders of Jesus' time conspired to sentence Christ to death to preserve their positions with the Romans: *"nor do you consider that it is expedient for us* that one *man should die for the people, and not that the whole nation should perish"* (John 11:50). Likewise, these black leaders have conspired to sentence millions and millions of innocent babies to death so that they might enjoy lifestyles of the rich and prestigious and the approval of their own Romans—the Democrat Party. *"They even sacrificed their sons and their daughters to demons, and shed innocent blood, the blood of their sons and daughters, whom they sacrificed to the idols of Canaan; And the land was polluted with blood"* (Psalm 106:37–38).

Just as the Romans tasked the religious leaders of Jesus' time with keeping the Jews subservient, so the Democrats have tasked these so-called leaders with keeping the black community in a position of servitude. These modern-day slave masters believe, like their predecessors, that the natural state of the black man is one of servitude. Thus, when men such as Dr. Alan Keyes, Dr. Ben Carson, Colonel Alan West, or Reverend Jesse Lee Peterson attempt to open the eyes of the black community, these so-called leaders, in defense of the Democrats' property, immediately begin a campaign of attack against them. *"So truth fails, and he who departs from evil makes himself a prey Then the Lord saw it, and it displeased Him that there was no justice"* (Isa. 59:15).

They have even stooped so low as to use the day meant to honor Martin Luther King Jr., as an opportunity to spread racial division. It is shameful that a day meant to honor a man who opposed racism is now used by professional racists as a tool to further racism. But such is the way of those on the left, who are experts at taking those things meant for good and perverting them. They know that should the eyes of the black community be opened to the destruction the policies the Democrat Party has wrought; the Democrats would no longer have any use for them. *"If we let Him alone like this, everyone will believe in Him, and the Romans will come and take away both our place and nation"* (John 11:48). These black leaders could teach the slaveholders of the past a few things about how to exploit a people.

And what of we who continue to support them even while they support and enact policies that we say we oppose. For over fifty years we have been doing what Michelle Obama recently commanded, "don't think, vote Democrat," she ordered. No matter who they are or what they stand for, we have put their election ahead of our beliefs, our well-being and the well-being and future of our children, that's the type of love that Abraham and Job reserved for God.

How long will we continue to count success as seeing these traitors live the lifestyles of the rich and famous while we continue to languish in poverty, illiteracy, and unemployment? I would say that these leaders' actions amount to stabbing us in the back, but they don't have to resort to that; they are comfortable stabbing us in the front, knowing that no matter what they do or say, just as Michelle Obama suggested, we'll vote for them anyway. While homosexuals have demanded a state-sanctioned redefinition of marriage and the citizens of Mexico have demanded that our immigrations laws be ignored and that they be granted US citizenship, we, the black community, have asked for nothing and received nothing in return. We continue to believe the generations-old lie that the Democrats have our best interest at heart. One report even finds that black men are no better off today than we were forty years ago.[23] These black leaders have used us to get them elected, while homosexuals, Mexican citizens, and those in the business of carrying out Margaret Sanger's vision for blacks, get the true benefits of their representation. As for us, we get rhetoric, while homosexuals, Mexican citizens, and child murderers get results. Even the chickens destined for KFC's fryers are better represented by these black leaders than black Americans are. Those on the left hand have asked for our children and, in exchange for power, position, and the praise of men, our black leaders have complied.

Give us your children. Give us their minds. Give us your children. Reject the divine (commandments of God).

Give us your children, for an education, for we specialize, in indoctrination.

Give us your children. We'll put them in class. We'll dumb it way down (lessons) to ensure that they pass.

Entrust to us, their education. Forget that we have (for them), such low expectations.

Give us your children, that's what you MUST do. No need to think, WE'LL do that for you.

Give us your children. Let US decide. Your sons should have husbands; your daughters have brides.

Give us your children, their hopes and their thoughts, the young AND the unborn, the entire lot.

Give us your children, surrender YOUR will, your freedoms we'll take, your future (children) we'll kill.

Give us your children (sons and daughters), your nephews and nieces, then you'll have earned, your thirty pieces (of silver).

CHAPTER 4

BARACK HUSSEIN OBAMA

"Now I beseech you, brethren, mark them which cause divisions and offences contrary to the doctrine which ye have learned; and avoid them. For they that are such serve not our Lord Jesus Christ, but their own belly; and by good words and fair speeches deceive the hearts of the simple" (Romans 16:17–18).

BARACK HUSSEIN OBAMA

*"Shall the throne of iniquity, which devises evil by law, Have
fellowship with You?"*
(Ps. 94:20)

F inally, we come to Barack Hussein Obama, a man who zealously
supports the legalized murder of unborn babies with a fervor
few others have demonstrated, except perhaps Hillary Clinton,
a man who effectively calls the God of creation's definition of
marriage discriminatory, a man who effectively calls Jesus Christ
a liar by claiming that Christ is not necessary for salvation, a man
who brazenly seeks to instruct the God of creation on matters of life
and morality—a man who is the President of the United States of
America. *"Shall the one who contends with the Almighty correct Him?
He who rebukes God, let him answer it"* (Job 40:2).

When Obama was elected, many in the black community cried
tears of joy at the election of the first African-American president.
Obama has continually attacked not only the future of the black
community through his strident promotion of child murder, but also
the God that we in the black community claim to serve. He continues
the long Democrat tradition of using blacks as a tool to get elected.
But his true passions lie in being favorably viewed by and openly
favoring Muslims, promoting the murder of unborn and newly born
babies, and promoting the lifestyle of Sodom and Gomorrah.

He has stated that the primary mission of NASA is now to
improve relations with the Muslim world—not sending astronauts

on space missions to explore outer space.[1] When Muslims wanted to build a victory mosque at the site of Ground Zero, Obama sided with them, not the families of the 9/11 victims.[2]

He has used taxpayer dollars to promote the murder of the unborn not only domestically but internationally as well. Whether it's through one of the deceptively named United Nations organizations or the $23,000,000 taxpayer dollars that he *illegally* gave to a group promoting two of his three loves, the murder of the unborn, and Sharia law, in Kenya.[3] Obama has made the murder of the unborn, much like the promotion of the lifestyle of Sodom and Gomorrah, a matter of foreign policy. These are the issues that are near and dear to Obama's heart, and he has applied America's limited treasures to promoting them, domestically and internationally. *"For where your treasure is, there your heart will be also"* (Matt. 6:21).

When he was a senator, Obama, criticizing then-President Bush, declared that raising the nation's debt limit was "irresponsible and unpatriotic."[4] Now it seems that every couple of months he is asking Congress to raise the debt ceiling.

Hypocritically, he claims that he is committed to creating more jobs and lessening the nation's support on foreign oil. Yet, when he was given the opportunity to do both with one act—by approving the Keystone Pipeline from Canada—he declined, inventing nonsensical reasons for why it should be postponed until after the 2012 election because he did not want to lose the support of environmentalists (Parsons and Richter 2011). Here we are in 2016 and the president still opposes the Keystone pipeline. It is obvious to those with eyes to see that the only job Obama was interested in saving was his own.

CERTIFYING OBAMA'S CHRISTIANITY

"Therefore by their fruits you will know them –
(Matt. 7:20).

E ven before BHO was elected, some people wondered whether he was a terrorist Trojan horse. Since his election, he has done little to demonstrate otherwise. BHO has been perhaps the biggest supporter of Islamic terrorists aside from Iran. He has continuously made excuses for the actions of terrorists, always finding a way to blame Americans or guns instead.

After terrorists murdered four Americans in Benghazi, BHO and Hillary Clinton spent a significant amount of taxpayer dollars apologizing to the terrorists and had no qualms about blaming a film maker for the actions of American hating terrorists. They then proceeded to continually lie to the families of the victims. When Islamic terrorists murdered one hundred thirty people in Paris, BHO referred to the murders as a setback. He did not display the passion that he saves for condemning America's policemen when they are forced to defend themselves against criminals and mobs. And while the Parisians were mourning the slaughter of one hundred thirty innocents, BHO released five Islamic terrorists from Guantanamo (West, 2015). Even after the terrorist attacks of San Bernardino, BHO pressured the FBI and National Security Council (NSC), to downplay the terrorism link (Bennett, 2015) just as he did in the case of Islamic terrorist, Major Nidal Hassan. This same Obama who immediately accuses police officers of wrongdoing before knowing the whole story continually rushes to the defense of Islam when it's most violent adherents slaughter Americans. After numerous reports that Orlando nightclub murderer had called 911 to express his allegiance to ISIS, our brilliant commander in chief remains baffled concerning the Islamic terrorist's motives. Ever at the ready to defend the image of Islam, Mr. Obama stated, "We've reached no definitive judgment on the precise motivations of the killer" (Limbaugh, 2016). And as expected, he immediately took to blaming the murders on guns (Limbaugh, 2016) and insinuated that Americans' attitudes towards homosexuals was partly to blame (Podhoretz, 2016). No mention of Islam's views on homosexuals. I wait to see now if, and how, he'll respond to reports that Mateen himself was a homosexual (Fox News, 2016). It may be that BHO is well aware of these reports, as according to TMZ, Mateen's ex-wife was advised by the FBI to "to keep mum about Mateen's homosexuality in interviews with American media."

BHO is quick to ask us to not blame all Muslims for the actions of a few, should he not take his own advice and not blame all gun owners for the actions of a few? As one commentator wondered, will the democrats seek to ban planes and pressure cookers as well? And what of knives, machetes, ball bearings, or any of the other devices that terrorists use to commit mass murder?

That said, I do think that the Democrats' proposal of banning those on no-fly lists from gun ownership and requiring background checks at gun shows are sensible proposals. Unfortunately, I also believe that this may be another example of liberals using a tragedy to their advantage; and, more importantly, I find it extremely hard to trust liberals after the deceptions of Obamacare. I suspect that any gun control laws put forth by these masters of deception would be turned around to abuse law abiding citizens and have little effect on those it was meant to stop.

While BHO's administration does not hesitate to consider pro-lifers, veterans, and evangelicals as terrorists, he attempts to move heaven and earth to deny that Islamic terrorists exist. BHO's administration has taken away the tools that our law and intelligence agencies might use to identify potential terrorist threats; he seeks every opportunity to release the dangerous terrorist at Guantanamo bay, 33 percent of whom return to the battlefield.[5] And this American president has given the biggest state sponsor of terrorism, Iran, the green light and billions of dollars to build a nuclear weapon.

BHO is determined to import hundreds of thousands of Muslim Syrian refugees to America. It matters not that there are confirmed reports of an ISIS operative stating that ISIS would use the refugee crisis to infiltrate western nations,[6] or that House Homeland Security Committee Chairman, Representative Michael McCaul, stated that there is evidence that ISIS terrorists would attempt to gain entry into the US through the Syrian refugee program,[85] or that the FBI has stated that there is no way to vet the Syrian refugees,[7] BHO is determined to bring thousands of potential Islamic terrorists to the US.

His love for Islam takes precedence over the safety of the American people. BHO's idea of rigorous vetting is to simply ask those from terrorist countries whether or not they are terrorists, like they did with San Bernardino murderer Tashfeen Malik. And while this self-professed Christian is determined to import hundreds of thousands of Muslims to America, he has denied entry to Christian refugees who are being murdered, beheaded, and crucified in the name of Islam. According to Geller, a mere fifty-two Syrian Christians have been allowed entry into the US by the Obama administration.

The greatest fear of his attorney general, Loretta Lynch, is that Americans might say something negative about Muslims, after two of their number, once again, slaughtered innocent Americans. Lynch, like her boss, is not concerned about the safety of Americans and has vowed to prosecute anyone who speaks negatively of Islam.[8] This makes BHO and Lynch of the same mentality as those who murdered twelve people at the offices of *Charlie Hebdo* magazine. If the subject is Islam, you have no right to freedom of speech.

Despite BHO's blatant hostility towards Christians and the Jewish state, many are willing to certify his Christianity and condemn those who believe otherwise. In a speech he gave in 2008 while in Cairo, BHO proclaimed, "The sweetest sound I know is the Muslim call to prayer" (Jackson, 2013). In 2012 at the UN, once again seeming to make excuses for Islamic terrorists after they had murdered twelve people at the office of French satirical magazine *Charlie Hebdo*, he stated, "The future must not belong to those who slander the prophet of Islam," and in his book, *The Audacity of Hope*, he declared, "I will stand with the Muslims should the political winds shift in an ugly direction."[9] And while he has been consumed with defending Islam and the terrorists that act in its name, he has displayed nothing but disdain and hatred for Christians.

Almost immediately after being elected, this supposed Christian began targeting those who believe in life, morality, country, and Christ. As early as 2009, the Obama Department of Homeland Security (DHS) issued a report advising law enforcement agencies to be on the look-out for so-called right-wing extremists.[10] Counted among these right-wing extremists were those who wanted our immigration laws enforced, those who believed in our constitutional right to bear arms, those who believe that murdering unborn children is in fact murdering unborn children, and military veterans who have willingly put their very lives on the line to defend America's freedoms.

It would seem that in the eyes of BHO and the Democrats these groups are far worse than the non-existent Islamic terrorists of Al Queda, the Taliban, and ISIS. In fact, it's been discovered that BHO's Department of Defense has been making the claim that members of the military, evangelical Christians, Catholics, and Orthodox Jews are no different from terror groups such as Hamas and Al Qaeda.[11] According to Newman, BHO's most recent attempt at targeting Christians is the appointment of a terrorism czar to monitor threats from Christians and those with anti-government views (those who disagree with his horrible polices). BHO has also joined with the modern-day Tower of Babel, the UN, in an effort to stamp out "anti-Muslim bigotry" wherever it may be hiding.[12] Like the dragon of Revelation, this antichrist wages a continuous war on Christians. *And the dragon was enraged with the woman, and he went to make war with the rest of her offspring, who keep the commandments of God and have the testimony of Jesus Christ.* (Rev. 12:17).

Still, most black Christians continue to support and defend him in his attacks on morality, life, and Christ. Given BHO's actions and statements, is it any wonder that many believe he is a Muslim? Donald Trump was widely condemned by the media, Democrats and Republicans for not coming to BHO's defense when one of his supporters called BHO a Muslim. Hillary Clinton, Lindsey Graham, and Chris Christie all had disparaging remarks because Trump did not, like John McCain before him, come to BHO's defense.[13] It's obvious that these liberals not only oppose free speech but also the freedom of thought. It is not Donald Trump's place to defend an anti-Christ who has displayed zero evidence of Christianity (*Therefore by their fruits you will know them* – Matt. 7:20) and should not American citizens be free to believe what they please? Obviously not in the eyes of the liberal thought police.

It should come as no surprise that those who refuse to surrender their thoughts and opinions to the liberal uni-mind are still unconvinced that BHO has America's best interests at heart. He is only interested in following our constitution when he is attempting to illegally convey its rights to foreigners and Islamic terrorists not entitled to constitutional protections. His strategy for combating terrorism includes releasing some of the deadliest terrorists back onto the battlefield, disarming law-abiding Americans, empowering the greatest state sponsor of terrorism, Iran, attending a climate conference (that must really scare the terrorists!), and prosecuting Americans who dare to say anything that does not portray Muslims in a positive light. I have to believe that an Islamic terrorist Trojan horse could not have been more successful at weakening America and strengthening Islamic terrorists than BHO has been.

When he declared to the nation that ISIS, this J. V. team, was contained, ISIS members murdered at least 127 people in Paris. As police in San Bernardino were searching for the Islamic terrorists who carried out an ISIS-style attack that killed fourteen Americans, BHO, in a CNN interview, assured the nation that Americans were safe from just such an attack.[14] At times it seems that Baghdad Bob is running the country.

ACTS OF OBAMA

*"O full of all deceit and all fraud, you son of the devil, you
enemy of all righteousness, will you not cease perverting the
straight ways of the Lord"
(Acts 13:10)?*

U nder the Obama administration, the US Constitution appears
to be null and void. He has openly declared that he will do
his will regardless of any objections by the Congress, in clear
violation of the Constitution's mandate of separation of powers.
When he launched the attacks on Libya, he did so at the behest of the
Arab League, and though he consulted with NATO, Obama ignored
the American Congress. Will we ever see another American president
who has the best interests of America at heart? Bill Clinton seemed
interested in pleasing the Chinese; George W. Bush sometimes acted
as if the citizens of Mexico were his constituents; and Barack Obama
acts as though he represents the interests of Arab and Muslim nations
all while he continues to thumb his nose at the American people and
our Constitution. He has appointed himself king and there seems
to be few who are willing to oppose him. *"Then the king shall do
according to his own will: he shall exalt and magnify himself above every
god, shall speak blasphemies against the God of gods, and shall prosper
till the wrath has been accomplished; for what has been determined shall
be done"* (Dan. 11:36).

I sometimes find myself wondering these days: *Whose America
is this anyway?* In some of our schools, the American flag has been

banned to keep from offending Mexican students.[94] Many of our country's founding documents aren't included in the educational curriculum because they are deemed "unconstitutional."[15] And now, someone who doesn't know anything about you or your situation gets to tell you from whom you can purchase health insurance.

In the topsy-turvy morality of the Obama administration, right has become wrong and wrong has become right. Law-breakers are given a pass and not prosecuted while the court system is used to persecute the righteous. Despite overwhelming evidence, Obama's corrupt Department of Justice (DOJ) dismissed an obvious case of voter intimidation against the New Black Panther Party in Philadelphia during the 2008 presidential election.[16]

Protecting the Illegal Immigrants and the Black Race-Destroying Planned Parenthood

When American states try to protect their citizens from the crime and financial expenses related to *illegal* immigration, Obama's DOJ sides with the citizens of other nations and sues the American states for trying to protect their citizens' jobs and lives.[17] When states tried to free themselves from the financial burdens and murderous results of funding Margaret Sanger's Planned Parenthood, Obama, the staunch advocate for legalized child murder, rides to the rescue of the organization founded explicitly to rid America of blacks.[18] And when it appeared that the child murderers would finally be brought to justice for a range of illegal deeds, including defrauding the government and covering up cases of statutory rape, one of Obama's appointees, Secretary of Health and Human Services, Kathleen Sebelius, shredded documents that implicated Planned Parenthood in the commission of these crimes.[19]

When the legislature agreed that no tax dollars should be granted to the corrupt community organizers of ACORN, Obama and the Justice Department, led by Attorney General Eric Holder, sought to circumvent the legislators and continue to fund the criminal actions of ACORN.[20]

Fast and Furious and the Radical Firearms Agenda

The Obama administration trotted Hillary Clinton out in front of the nation to declare that American guns were the major cause of violence in the Mexican drug trade. [21] Several months later, the nation would discover that the Obama administration had in fact delivered over 1,000 guns to Mexican drug dealers as part of an operation called "Fast and Furious," a program by which the administration funneled thousands of guns to Mexican drug cartels in what I firmly believe was an attempt to curtail our Second Amendment rights. [22] At least one of these guns would later be tied to the murder of a US border patrol agent; others are said to have been used to murder thousands of Mexican citizens. [23] Most of the others remain unaccounted for. Many believe that the administration would use these guns as an excuse to ban personal gun ownership in America.

In the aftermath of the murders of at least two US agents, this gun-running scheme has backfired and led to investigations into the Fast and Furious operation. During that period, Attorney General Eric Holder and the Obama administration held no one responsible. To this day no one has been held responsible.

Exploiting Tragedies for the Gun Control Agenda

Whereas Fast and Furious did not give the administration the fuel to restrict or ban gun ownership in America in clear violation of the Second Amendment, the random senseless shootings in Aurora, Colorado (at a film screening), and Oak Creek, Wisconsin (at a Sikh temple), have provided the administration with a crisis that, according to their mantra, they would not let *go to waste*.

In January of 2016, BHO finally made good on using an executive order in an attempt at gun control.[24] The fact that his executive orders were not more wide ranging leads me to believe that this was more of an effort to create a distraction from the terror attacks of San Bernardino and more importantly from the fact that BHO was about to release even more terrorists from Guantanamo. BHO's supposed concern for those killed or injured in gun-related crimes has somewhat of a hollow ring when one considers that prosecutions of gun crimes is down by 40 percent under his administration.[25] Adding more doubt to BHO's sincerity is the fact that he has released 36,000 violent criminal illegal immigrants (WND, 2014). Counted among them are murderers, rapists, kidnappers, and drug dealers (WND, 2014).

Displaying his disdain for America's sovereignty, in December 2009 Obama gave Interpol, a European police force, authority over Americans, over state and local law enforcement, over the FBI, our courts, and the US Congress (McCarthy, 2009).

In 2008, when Khalid Sheikh Mohammed, the self-proclaimed mastermind of the 9/11 terror attacks, and four co-defendants were prepared to plead guilty to the charges brought against them, the newly elected Obama halted the proceedings while his DOJ attorneys, many of whom had previously represented Gitmo terrorists pro bono, sought to have the guilty plea thrown out, citing torture.[26]

Healthcare Bribery

In acts of open bribery, the Obama administration bribed representatives from Nebraska, Louisiana, and Florida with American taxpayers' money to ensure the passage of his healthcare reform legislation (the so-called Affordable Care Act, or Obamacare). These acts became known as the "Cornhusker Kickback," the "Louisiana Purchase," and the "Florida Flim-Flam".[27]

Bribery of Joe Sestak

In yet another act of bribery, Obama enlisted the aid of Bill Clinton to help bribe Congressman Joe Sestak to refrain from running for senate against the personification of the Republican establishment, Arlen Specter. Sestak was offered a high-ranking position in the administration if he would drop his primary challenge against Republican-turned-Democrat Arlen Specter. [28]

Questionable Legitimacy--Birth Certificate and Social Security Number

After spending millions of dollars to conceal his actual birth certificate for over two years, after intense pressure from Donald Trump, Obama finally released what some experts have described as a fraudulent Photo-Shopped copy. Even his Social Security Number presents more questions than answers as it appears to have been issued to a resident of Connecticut, a state in which Obama never lived. In spite of these discrepancies, a spineless Congress, complicit courts, and a pro-Obama media continue to provide cover for Obama (Baldwin, 2010).

Weakening the Superpower

Under the leadership of BHO, this superpower, America, has become a super puppet. When the Russians decided that America should scrap plans for a missile shield for herself and her allies, Obama agreed. And six months before the 2012 presidential election, somehow positive that he would indeed be re-elected, Obama was overheard on an open microphone telling outgoing Russian President Dmitri Medvedev to let Vladimir Putin know that he would have "more flexibility" concerning the missile shields after he was re-elected (Tapper, 2012). In early 2014, the Russians, after annexing Crimea, laughed at Obama's empty threats and meaningless sanctions of 11 people. I am sure that they, like most of the world, took note of Obama's ineffectual "red line" concerning the massacre in Syria involving the use of chemical weapons.

Benghazi Consulate Attack: When Americans in Benghazi, Libya, were fighting for their lives against radical Islamic terrorists, the Obama administration not only refused to send them aid but also ordered those who were willing to help to do nothing (Tapper and Bash, 2013). Afterwards, the Obama administration apologized to the terrorists and vowed to arrest the one responsible for the attack, not the terrorists themselves, but a man who had produced a film that showed Islam, the so-called "religion of peace," for what it truly is—a religion of violence (Noe, 2012). *If a ruler pays attention to lies, all his servants become wicked* (Prov. 29:12).

Knowing full well that this was a terrorist attack, the administration proceeded to trot out Susan Rice to lie about the attack and blame a film maker and not the terrorists in a deliberate attempt to cover up the administration's bungled handling of the attack and advance the administration's narrative that Obama had won the war on terror in the face of the imminent 2012 election (Kiely, 2014). Suspected of knowing that Sergeant Beau Bergdahl was a deserter, the Obama administration dispatched Susan Rice out to continue her habit of lying, by claiming that the deserter, Bergdahl, had served the country with honor and distinction (Lucas, 2015).

Always looking for an opportunity to set the terrorists at Guantanamo free, Obama made a secret deal with the Taliban to free five senior Taliban terrorists in exchange for deserter Sergeant Beau Bergdahl. Six American soldiers lost their lives while searching for Bergdahl who voluntarily walked away from his post and into the arms of the Taliban. For Bergdahl's act of honor and distinction, according to Susan Rice, a rose garden ceremony was held to announce his release.

Just as with the "Fast and Furious" operation, and questions about the IRS' targeting of conservative and pro-Israel groups, questions about Benghazi have gone unanswered and no one has been held accountable.

And then there's Obama's signature piece of legislation, which I like to call "Hell's Care Reform," whereby Obama blatantly lied to the American people in ensuring them that they would be able to keep their present doctors and their present insurance carriers. The lack of any true consequences for their actions seems only to have emboldened the Obama administration, for Obama and his minions have no qualms over using executive orders to carry out his radical left-wing agenda. It seems that our Constitution and our Congress mean very little to this worst president in America's history. Not only is BHO the worst president in the history of the United States, but he also appears to be the most delusional. In a June 2015 speech, BHO claimed that under his administration the US has been returned to world dominance (Houck, 2015). Perhaps, believing that he has the power to speak things into existence, he makes this ridiculous statement while Russian President Putin continues to claim property, the Iranians continue to pursue atomic weaponry, with BHO's approval, China has taken to telling America where we can and cannot go in international waters, and ISIS continues to murder, behead, and burn countless victims all while claiming territory for their Islamic caliphate. In another illustration of this president's delusion or arrogance, perhaps both, he proudly claims Yemen as a success of his counter terrorism strategy, all while the Yemeni president has been forced to flee the presidential palace (Hughes, 2015).

After having surrendered all of the gains that the Bush administration achieved in Iraq, by telling terrorists when the US would be withdrawing troops, BHO, the blameless one, blames former President Bush for the creation of his J. V. team, ISIS (Lucas, 2015). Displaying both his arrogance and hypocrisy, this most divisive president in the nation's history had the gall to lecture a group of young Asian fellows on the importance of non-discrimination and the avoidance of divisive politics, acts that he claimed he would never participate in (Hamner, 2015). This is the same man who has called Americans arrogant, constantly complains of white privilege, has openly shown his disdain for Christians and Jews, and seeks every opportunity to label police officers as racists for daring to confront suspects and criminals who happen to be black.

OBAMA'S APPOINTMENTS

"When an unclean spirit goes out of a man, he goes through dry places, seeking rest, and finds none. Then he says, 'I will return to my house from which I came.' And when he comes, he finds it empty, swept, and put in order. Then he goes and takes with him seven other spirits more wicked than himself, and they enter and dwell there; and the last state of that man is worse than the first. So shall it also be with this wicked generation"
(Matt. 12:43–45).

Many had viewed the Clinton administration as the most corrupt presidential administration in the history of the US. During the Clinton years we saw US military secrets disclosed to the Chinese in exchange for monetary donations to the Clinton administration from the Chinese military. Under the Clinton administration the Chinese gained the technology to launch missile strikes against the US (Lincoln, 2003).

But the Clinton administration now pales in comparison to the administration Obama assembled. It was Obama himself who said that we should judge him by the people that he surrounded himself with. So let's do just that.

Obama's faith adviser, Eboo Patel, a Muslim, equated American Christians with the terrorists of Al Queda. This same man also called American freedom and equality a myth. Indeed, under BHO this freedom and equality are in danger of becoming extinct, but that was not Patel's meaning. Patel also stated that if he had the opportunity he might have joined Obama friend and terrorist Bill Ayers in the 1960s (Klein, 2011).

Richard Holbrook (the Afghanistan Czar) is an advocate for the legalized murder of unborn babies (abortion), legalized drug use, and wants to dissolve the Second Amendment ("right to bear arms").

Ed Montgomery (the Auto Recovery Czar) is a promoter of reverse racism who believes that world poverty is caused by successful US businesses. He is a member of the Communist Dubois Club and a board member of the corrupt community organizers group ACORN.

Jeffrey Crowley (the AIDS Czar) is an adherent to the lifestyle of Sodom and Gomorrah who supports the perversion of the God-ordained institution of marriage and believes that those who practice the lifestyle of Sodom and Gomorrah should have special rights, including free health care.

Alan Bersin (the Border Czar) has proven to be very successful, *if* you don't believe in borders. As the border Czar under Janet Reno, Bersin has proven his record of fending off all efforts to close America's borders and enforce our immigration laws.

David Hayes (California's Water Czar) is an environmentalist with absolutely no training in water management. Environmentalists share Obama's vision of keeping US dollars flowing to those nations that hate the United States. These nations use the money we pay them for oil to plot our destruction.

Dennis Ross (Central Region Czar) is a passionate advocate for murdering unborn babies (abortion) who believes that US policy is to blame for wars in the Middle East. Ross would outlaw Americans' right to own firearms if it were in his power to do so.

Lynn Rosenthal (Domestic Violence Czar) is a radical feminist who supports male castration.

Gil Kerlikowske (Drug Czar), ironically, supports the legalization of drugs and the outlawing of firearms in America.

Paul Volcker (Economic Czar) is yet another proven failure on the team. Volcker served as the head of the Federal Reserve under Jimmy Carter. Under Volcker's previous leadership stint, the US economy nearly collapsed irrevocably. I would garner that Obama is hoping that Volcker will be more successful this time in causing a complete collapse of the US economy.

Cameron Davis (Great Lakes Czar) is another environmentalist and also a race baiter. Davis accuses George Bush of poisoning the water that minorities have to drink. Perhaps if Mr. Bush would join the Democrats in promoting the legalized murders of millions of unborn black children and trapping them in violent under performing schools Davis would have a better opinion of him. Like another water management czar, Davis has absolutely no training in water management and is a former member of the criminal organization ACORN.

Van Jones (Green Jobs Czar) is an avowed communist who is a "9/11 truther" who believes that George Bush caused 9/11 and should be investigated for war crimes. After Sean Hannity exposed his views and statements, Mr. Jones eventually resigned from public service, but I wouldn't be surprised if he is still involved in the Obama administration behind the scenes.

Daniel Fried (Guantanamo Closure Czar), like Eric Holder and other members of Obama's Department of Justice, is an advocate for freeing foreign terrorists. Like Obama's pastor Rev. Jeremiah Wright, Fried believes that America is to blame for 9/11. He believes that terrorists deserve rights above and beyond those of American citizens.

Nancy Anne DeParle (Health Czar) is a strong advocate for the rationing of health care.

Dennis Blair (Intelligence Czar) is a retired navy man who, ironically, opposed the US guided missile program because he felt that it was too provocative. Blair is yet another member of the Council on Foreign Relations who blames the US for regional wars.

George Mitchell (Mideast Peace Czar), like Obama, is an enemy of Israel and believes that it should be split up into two or three smaller plots—no doubt to make it easier for her terrorist enemies to complete Hitler's final solution. While Mitchell is anti-gun, he supports special rights for those who live the lifestyle of Sodom and Gomorrah.

Cass Sunstein (Regulatory Czar) is a liberal activist judge who believes that free speech should be limited for the common good. Sunstein opposes personal freedoms such as the right to bear arms.

John Holdren (Science Czar) is an environmentalist with absolutely no science training. Mr. Holdren blames US businesses for world poverty.

Earl Devaney (Stimulus Accountability Czar) has devoted his career to eliminating Americans' right to bear arms. He believes that the citizens of Mexico are entitled to freely claim everything that taxpaying American citizens have worked hard to achieve. It was Mr. Devaney who proclaimed that US firearms stores are to blame for the drug wars in Mexico.

J. Scott Gration (Sudan Czar) is a native of the Republic of the Congo who believes that the US does very little to help third world countries. Despite the fact that the US is the major financial supporter of the undermining UN, Gration wants the US citizens to be taxed even more in order to support this modern-day tower of Babel, the UN

Herb Allison (TARP Czar) is yet another proven failure. Allison's decision to use real estate mortgages to back up the US stock market was a major catalyst in causing the United States' plunge into a recession and caused millions to lose their life savings to underwrite the TARP program.

Ashton Carter (Weapons Czar) wants all privately owned weapons in the US confiscated and destroyed. Like our good friends at the UN, Carter believes that American citizens should not be able to own guns. His sole purpose is eliminating American citizen's right to bear arms.

Gary Samore (WMD Policy Czar) is a communist who wants the US to unilaterally destroy all of her WMD as a show of good faith to her enemies. Like the weapons Czar, he has no other purpose but to see our nation disarmed and at the mercy of her enemies (DeSantis, 2012).

And then there is **Dan Savage**, Obama's appointee to the Commission Against Bullying. Mr. Savage, a champion of the lifestyle of Sodom and Gomorrah, recently called the God of creation's views on that lifestyle bulls**t (Akin, 2012).

Even the homosexual pedophiles of NAMBLA were well represented in Obama's administration as he appointed **Kevin Jennings** as his Safe School Czar. Jennings is the founder of GLSEN, a group that seeks to normalize homosexuality and teaches young people that disagreeing with the homosexual promotion is a form of oppression. As a school teacher, Jennings encouraged the homosexual relationship of a fifteen-year-old student with an older man. Instead of turning in the adult, as teachers are required to do, Jennings suggested that condoms be used (Bauer, 2011).

Eric Holder

Then we have Eric Holder, former Attorney General of the United States, a man who came into the position with a history of corruption already on his résumé. As Bill Clinton's Deputy Attorney General, Holder was accused of participating in a plan to keep the DOJ from finding out about, and opposing, a pardon for fugitive financier Marc Rich. The whole unsavory affair came to be regarded as a selling of pardons by the Clinton Administration; an affair in which Eric Holder played a pivotal role (Baram, 2008). In 1997 this same Eric Holder offered some of his fellow Democrats' recommendations on how members of the FALN terrorist group could be granted clemency (Cohen, 2008). Time has done little to diminish Holder's love for the enemies of America. Before becoming Attorney General of the US, Mr. Holder worked for a legal agency that freely offered its services to help free terrorists held at Guantanamo. And when Holder became America's chief law enforcement officer, he brought some of his fellow terrorist sympathizers with him, leading many to call the DOJ the Department of Jihad (McCarthy, 2010).

Professing himself to be an agent of law and order, Holder has merely picked up where he left off during his time with the Clinton administration. He has not ceased in his efforts to undermine America. Whether fighting on the side of terrorists or preventing states from enacting and enforcing immigration laws and ensuring legitimate voting rolls, he and the Obama administration continually showed their disdain and hatred for America. Obama and the democrats speak of freedom, liberty, and equality as all while they implement policies and laws designed to strip them away. *"While they promise them liberty, they themselves are slaves of corruption; for by whom a person is overcome, by him also he is brought into bondage"* (2 Peter 2:19).

Hillary Clinton

Finally, we have Hillary Clinton, BHO's former secretary of state and the presumptive 2016 heir to the liberal throne. As secretary of state Mrs. Clinton brought with her a history of scandals and corruption. Along with her husband Bill, the Clinton's have long been suspected of selling America's security and secrets for power and personal gain. In *10 Scandals Involving Hillary Clinton You May Have*

Forgotten, Fox (2015) outlines some of the scandals from Hillary Clinton's past. Some of the allegations involve the willingness to sell lucrative positions to the Chinese in exchange for financial donations (Chinagate), the brazen theft of white house furniture when Bill's presidency was over (Lootergate), the White Water scandal, which involved allegations of improper campaign contributions, financial favors and fraud. Other scandals included Travelgate, in which Hillary fired several government employees from the travel office and sought to replace them with friends and relatives (Fox, 2010). These days, as Hillary makes her presidential run, she is being dogged by controversies over the Benghazi attack, having a personal email server, and destroying evidence from it, and the appearance that she used her position as secretary of state to financially benefit the Clinton foundation. In support of the butchers in the child murder industry she constantly harps on the fictional war on women. Constantly insinuating that American women are denied certain rights, I'm still trying to figure out exactly what those rights are.

As for someone who is waging a war on women, Mrs. Clinton needs to look no farther than her own household. She and her husband have been waging a war on women for years. She has been less than kind to those women who have accused her husband of sexual assault. Author Roger Stone contends that Hillary Clinton has conducted a campaign of terror against those women who fell victim to her husband's sexual assaults (Wilde, 2015).

Mr. Stone, author of *The Clintons' War on Women,* presents Bill Clinton as a serial rapist whose crimes were covered up by Hillary Clinton and the media. The author contends that, on top of being sexually assaulted by Bill Clinton, his victims were also psychologically assaulted by Hillary Clinton. According to Stone, attempts at silencing Bill Clinton's victims included slashing tires, smashing windshields, killing pets, late night phone calls and veiled threats against the women's children (Wilde, 2015). And this woman is the person that most of the black Christians that I have spoken to support, unconditionally, for president.

The same Hillary Clinton who, along with many other Democrats, believes that the law should be used to force Christians to comply with policies and actions that go against the Christian faith. *Do not be unequally yoked together with unbelievers. For what fellowship has righteousness with lawlessness? And what communion has light with darkness? And what accord has Christ with Belial? Or what part has a believer with an unbeliever* (2 Cor. 6:14–15)? After disappointing outings in Iowa's and New Hampshire's Democratic presidential primaries, Clinton, proud recipient of the Margaret Sanger award and an admirer of this same Margaret Sanger who plotted to exterminate the entire black race (Ertelt, 2014), fully expected that it was blacks who would help her to win the party's nomination. During her acceptance speech for the Democrat Party's nomination for president, this admirer of Margaret Sanger voiced her desire to make the Democrat Party's death covenant with Planned Parenthood even more lucrative as she voiced her desire to eliminate any and all restrictions on murdering unborn children and to funnel even more taxpayer dollars to the child murderers.

To Mrs. Clinton, murdering the unborn is a social good (FRC, 2016). Society is benefited when those people that they don't want to many of are reduced or limited in their numbers. According to Margaret Sanger Blacks are those people. According to (Ertelt, 2016) Mrs. Clinton, in February 2016, defended the torturous partial-birth abortion procedure, where fully developed babies are stabbed in the head and have their brains suctioned out. During an interview on *The View*, Mrs. Clinton stated that unborn babies have no constitutional rights, not even the right to life. During a presidential forum at Drake University, Mrs. Clinton stated that the legal ability to murder unborn children was a "fundamental human right" (Ertelt, 2016).

And this is the woman who would be, and very well may be, president. She denies that babies have the most basic right, a right to life. However, she contends that ending the life of an unborn child (murder) is a "fundamental human right." And most black Christians will sing the virtues of this evil woman and her party who continues to carry out Margaret Sanger's vision for blacks. Thou they slay us, still will we trust them.

These are but some of the people President Obama wants us to judge him by. Many have absolutely no training in the fields over which he had appointed them. It would seem that the only qualification that Obama looks for is that these Czars be anti-American, anti-Israel, sympathetic to terrorists, anti-gun, anti-free speech, advocates for murdering unborn children, and promoters of the lifestyle of Sodom and Gomorrah. When Obama speaks of the jobs that he has created, think back on these czars, they and the thousands of new IRS agents that will be needed to punish those who fail to purchase insurance under Obama's healthcare reform, for these are the jobs the Obama administration has created. *"If a ruler pays attention to lies, all his servants become wicked"* (Prov. 29:12).

None of these individuals has been approved or confirmed by Congress, and even the former KKK member, the late Robert Byrd, was concerned about Obama's appointment of these individuals with no congressional oversight (Straub, 2009). But as the president has shown in almost every instance since his election, normal rules do not apply to him. Nor, it seems, is anyone willing to hold him accountable.

BARACK HUSSEIN OBAMA –
ENEMY OF CHRIST

"It was granted to him to make war with the saints and to overcome them. And authority was given him over every tribe, tongue, and nation"
(Rev. 13:7).

Not only should Christians judge Obama by those he surrounds himself with, as he asks, but scripture tells us that we will know the character of an individual by his works. *"You will know them by their fruits. Do men gather grapes from thornbushes or figs from thistles? Even so, every good tree bears good fruit, but a bad tree bears bad fruit"* (Matt. 7:16–17). And what can the black community say of the fruits Obama has produced and, by extension, the fruits of those who support him?

States that would rather support a culture of life have been forced to participate in funding the legalized murder of unborn babies. Those who believe in the God-ordained institution of marriage have suffered persecution, as this president and his supporters, the champions of tolerance, have characterized any who hold to the biblical definition of marriage as homophobic, bigoted, discriminatory, and, ironically, intolerant (Demarco, 2012).

And while many will say that Obama is hostile to religion, it seems that his hostility is reserved for one religion only: Christianity. While the president likes to claim he is a Christian, his policies, his appointees, and his very words are clearly anti-Christian. His is a Christianity in which Christ is not necessary, in which Jesus' divinity is denied (Snyder, 2013). *"For many deceivers have gone out into the world who do not confess Jesus Christ as coming in the flesh. This is a deceiver and an antichrist"* (2 John 1:7).

The unspoken creed of this administration, indeed of all those on the left, seems to be: smite the shepherd (outlaw all public expressions of Christianity) and the sheep will be scattered (the righteous will be silenced), then we will lay our hands on their little ones (murder the unborn and sexualize and pervert the morals of the young).

Can it be that we in the black community consider the destruction of innocent unborn lives, the perverting of the God-ordained institution of marriage, and constant attacks on Christ to be the fruits of a good tree? When white evangelical pastors criticized the president for claiming that Jesus Christ was not necessary for salvation, effectively calling Christ a liar, some prominent black pastors came to the president's defense, not Christ's (Meyer, 2008). *"I have come in My Father's name, and you do not receive Me; if another comes in his own name, him you will receive. How can you believe, who receive honor from one another, and do not seek the honor that comes from the only God"* (John 5:43–44)? Sadly, these pastors honor the president more than they honor the Lord Jesus.

During a prayer breakfast meant to reflect on the Easter holiday, in what seems like a veiled defense of the atrocities of ISIS, the Islamic terrorist group who *beheaded* Christians and burns people alive, Obama, *accuser of the brethren*, goes back over a thousand years to link Christians to the Crusades and the inquisitions (WorldNet Daily, 2015).

While marginalizing traditional days of Christian observances, such as the National Day of Prayer, even to the extent of remaining silent when Franklin Graham was dis-invited, he has made it a point to observe, celebrate, and participate in events related to Ramadan and anything that promotes the lifestyle of Sodom and Gomorrah (homosexuality). It is no surprise then that on at least three separate occasions this president has declared to the world that America is no longer a Christian nation. On that declaration, though, I must reluctantly agree with him. The separation of Christ and state, the murder of over 1 million unborn and newly born babies yearly, and the enlargement of the borders of Sodom and Gomorrah mark us as anything but a Christian nation. And during the Democratic National Committee's 2012 convention, the entire nation witnessed the Democrat Party reject the God of creation on not one but three successive occasions (Barber, 2012).

This telling rejection of God was reminiscent of when the Jews rejected Christ on three occasions when Pilate was determined to set him free, as seen in Matthew 27:20–23.

> *But the chief priests and elders persuaded the multitude that they should ask Barabbas, and destroy Jesus. The governor answered and said unto them, whether of the twain will ye that I release unto you? They said, Barabbas. Pilate saith unto them, what shall I do then with Jesus which is called Christ? They all say unto him, let him be crucified. And the governor said, Why, what evil hath he done? But they cried out the more, saying, let him be crucified" But the chief priests and elders persuaded the multitudes that they should ask for Barabbas and destroy Jesus. The governor answered and said to them "which of the two do you want me to release to you?" They said "Barabbas!" Pilate said to them "what then shall I do with Jesus who is called Christ?" they all said to him "Let him be crucified." Then the governor said "Why, what evil has he done?" But they cried out all the more saying, "Let him be crucified!"* (Matt. 27:20–23).

Inserted into their platform in the place of God was government (Barber, 2012). Elevating government over God is one of the defining characteristics of socialism. Socialism covets the property of others and ultimately steals the earnings of the industrious and gives it to others. Socialism is a blatant defiance of three of the Ten

Commandments—thou shalt have no other gods before me, thou shalt not covet, and thou shalt not steal. And while references to God and Jerusalem, the city of David, were ultimately reintroduced into the DNC's platform, it was not with the consent of the Democrats. Just as in Jesus' time, wise men of today continue to seek Him, and the wicked of today continue to seek His destruction, to deny his divinity, and to outlaw the very mention of His name. According to the Religious Freedom Coalition, Christians in the Middle East are suffering unprecedented persecution after the wave of revolutions that have recently taken place there. But, incredibly, the US is denying them refuge while encouraging the immigration of Muslims who they, the Obama administration, know have supported terrorism (Bruce, 2014).

When Obama assumed office, he and his administration immediately began providing cover for Islamic terrorists. When Army Major and Islamic terrorist Nidal Hasan murdered thirteen of America's military heroes while screaming Allah Akbar, Obama characterized it as "workplace violence." But the Aurora movie shootings he called terrorism. When Hasan murdered America's soldiers, Obama immediately cautioned Americans not to jump to conclusions that it was what was obvious to everyone but the Obama administration— another attack by an Islamic terrorist (Geller, 2012). On yet another occasion, unable to control his urge to defend the most violent of his Muslim brethren, BHO claimed that the lack of education and other opportunities drove young Sunnis to terrorism (Jager, 2015). If a lack of education and job opportunities forced people to commit acts of terrorism, blacks would have turned to terrorism years ago, and under the Obama administration would have been on a terrorist rampage as the unemployment rates for blacks continue to be the highest in the nation. Ever since 9/11 Islamic terrorists have never been shy about telling us why they hate and kill us, because their faith demands it. Yet, our brilliant leaders continue to correct the murderous terrorists and tell them, and us, that terrorism is caused by a lack of education and high unemployment.

When Islamic terrorists murdered Americans at the Libyan consulate in Benghazi, the Obama administration laid the blame squarely on the shoulders of filmmaker Sam Bacile instead of on the terrorists who carried out the attack. Bacile had made the mistake of thinking that free speech still existed in America and made a movie that did not show the Islamic faith in a particularly positive light. After the murder of our citizens in Libya, the Obama administration, predictably, trotted out representatives to characterize the murderous attacks as anything but terror related. Initially they characterized it as a spontaneous event, ignoring the crucial fact that the attacks occurred on the anniversary of 9/11 (Kessler, 2012). And as has been his custom since taking over the White House, Obama was quick to apologize to those who have murdered American citizens. Thus he condemned the makers of the anti-Islam film, but apologized to the Islamic terrorists (York, 2012).

But this has been the history of the Obama administration—apologizing to terrorists and condemning arrogant America. As I write this, none of those who murdered our ambassador and three other Americans have been held accountable but, just as Hillary Clinton promised, Sam Bacile has been arrested and consequently convicted on unrelated charges related to parole violation (Barnes, 2012).

After Islamic terrorist Muhammad Youssef Abdulazeez massacred four Marines in Chattanooga, Tennessee, not even a blog post in which the shooter praises the virtues of conducting "Jihad for the sake of Allah" was enough to give our brilliant leaders, and media, a clue as to what prompted the murders, as BHO, the FBI and the, media wondered aloud what could have driven the Jihadist to murderer American soldiers (Kant, 2015). The terrorist sympathizers in the media and the administration are quick to blame every police shooting on racism, before even hearing the facts, but when it comes to obvious Islamic terrorism, they quickly warn that we should not jump to conclusions.

According to BHOs administration, there are no such things as "Islamic terrorists." Terrorist attacks are now to be known as "man caused disasters" (Hanson, 2013). But, while the administration denied the existence of Islamic terrorists, the Department of Homeland Security (DHS) put out the word that nationwide law enforcement should be on the lookout for a different kind of terrorist. These new terrorists included US military veterans, gun owners, those who believed in the sovereignty of America, and those who wanted less government intrusion in their lives. Also counted on the Obama list of actual terrorists were those who believed in the God-ordained institution of marriage between males and females and those who believe that life begins at conception. And while conservatives were to be monitored, the free speech of pro-sharia law Muslims who criticized the US were to be ensured (Johnson, 2013). Imagine that, military veterans who have actually been fighting Islamic terrorists, and those who believe in life and traditional marriage are terrorists, while the likes of Hamas and the Muslim Brotherhood are honorable partners in seeking peace.

In a telling, and sad, commentary on the state of America's morality—perhaps *immorality* would be a better word, during the 2012 Republican presidential primaries, Democrats in Michigan turned out to support former Pennsylvania Senator Rick Santorum over Mitt Romney. Senator Santorum is a staunch defender of life for the unborn and the biblical definition of marriage. Republicans have also resorted to this measure in an attempt at helping the politically weaker of their opponents. The Democrats reasoning was that Obama would fare better in a contest against Santorum than he would against Romney, that the majority of Americans would throw their support behind an advocate for the murder of unborn babies and behind a champion of the lifestyle of Sodom and Gomorrah rather than support someone who holds Santorum's Christian worldview (Jacobs, 2012).

Sadly, they were probably right. Even the unprincipled Republican leadership, as evidenced by the way they distance themselves from evangelicals and conservatives in favor of more lukewarm (moderate/liberal) candidates, recognizes that in today's America anyone displaying a shred of biblical morality will receive little support. *"Should one who hates justice govern? Will you condemn Him who is most just* (Job 34:17)?

Even at that, however, I was surprised when Obama defeated Mitt Romney for the presidency in 2012. After the election many questioned what Romney had done wrong and speculated about what he should have done differently. I thought Romney ran a great campaign, unlike John McCain before him (who at times caused me to wonder if he was campaigning against or for Obama). McCain called Obama a decent man (Diakides, 2008), prohibited the mention of Obama's middle name "Hussein" (Luo, 2008), and even declared that any discussion of Obama's pastor, the Reverend Jeremiah Wright, was off limits (Ellerson, 2008). Even now I find myself once again wondering whose side Mr. McCain is on. While he never questioned BHO's eligibility, he has recently come out to question that of Ted Cruz (Unruh, 2016).

Romney's loss may have been a symptom of what we are seeing play out in the current election cycle; conservatives who are frustrated and disgusted with the lack of results from a Republican leadership that continues to betray them year after year. And while conservatives expect candidates to display honesty and morality, liberal Democrats seem to prefer a different kind of representative. When it was revealed that Connecticut senatorial candidate Richard Blumenthal had repeatedly lied about having fought in Vietnam, the voters couldn't wait to elect him (Hernandez, 2010). There have been a number of politicians that have lied about their military service in an underhanded attempt to gain an advantage over their opponents or to increase their standing in the public eye (Beutler, 2010). In the past such an outright lie would disqualify the individual in the public's eye.

Today, when candidates lie, especially Democrat candidates, they are elevated and adored. Republican candidates who resort to blatant lies are usually asked to step down or withdraw by their party, unless of course it's Lindsey Graham, who also repeatedly lied about being a Gulf War Veteran, with no apparent backlash (Pareen, 2010). When Massachusetts senatorial candidate Elizabeth Warren was accused of falsely identifying herself as a Native American in order to enhance her prospects of getting a job as a minority, she too was elected (Walsh, 2014). And when Hillary Clinton lied about being shot at in Bosnia it was referred to as a misstatement: Hillary misspoke; she didn't lie. She would later be appointed Secretary of State by her former opponent for the Democratic presidential nomination, Barack Obama (Beutler, 2010). And even after he and his representatives lied no fewer than 37 times that Americans would be able to keep their current doctors and health insurance plans (Holan, 2013), there were no consequences for these lies. *We the people* have become much like those the Apostle Paul identified in Romans 1:28–32. We reject the likes of Santorum, Bachman, Keyes, West, and Huckabee, men and women who boldly express biblical faith. But we embrace and defend liars, thieves, advocates for murder, and promoters of immorality.

"And even as they did not like to retain God in their knowledge, God gave them over to a debased mind, to do those things which are not fitting; being filled with all unrighteousness, sexual immorality, wickedness, covetousness, maliciousness; full of envy, murder, strife, deceit, evil-mindedness; they are whisperers, backbiters, haters of God, violent, proud, boasters, inventors of evil things, disobedient to parents, undiscerning, untrustworthy, unloving, unforgiving, unmerciful; who, knowing the righteous judgment of God, that those who practice such things are deserving of death, not only do the same but also approve of those who practice them (Rom. 1:28–32).

Under the influence of those on the left we have become a nation that loves evil and hates good. If you believe that Jesus Christ is the only way to salvation you may be called *intolerant* or *extreme*. *"Nor is there salvation in any other, for there is no other name under heaven given among men by which we must be saved"* (Acts 4:12). If you believe that children are gifts from God and not a punishment and that life begins at conception, you may be called *controversial, anti-choice,* or extreme. *"Behold, children are a heritage from the Lord, the fruit of the womb is a reward"* (Psalm 127:3). If you believe that marriage is the union of a male and female you will be called *homophobic,* be accused of hate speech, and probably lose your job, just as the newly appointed CEO of Mozilla, Brandon Eich, who in March 2014 was forced out of the company he had founded merely because he had contributed $1,000 to a campaign in support of California's Proposition 8, defining marriage as between a man and a woman back in 2008 (Kim, 2014). *"Therefore a man shall leave his father and mother and be joined to his wife, and they shall become one flesh"* (Gen. 2:24). And now, if you don't want men and boys going into the same restrooms as your wives and daughters, you are accused of discrimination. Under the influence of those on the left we have become a nation that calls good evil and evil good. *"Woe to those who call evil good, and good evil; Who put darkness for light, and light for darkness; Who put bitter for sweet, and sweet for bitter"* (Isaiah 5:20).

Perhaps more than anyone in recent history, Barack Hussein Obama personifies the verse of scripture that warns Christians of **wolves in sheep's clothing**. *"Beware of false prophets, who come to you in sheep's clothing, but inwardly they are ravenous wolves. You will know them by their fruits. Do men gather grapes from thornbushes or figs from thistles"* (Matt. 7:15–16)._

When teenager Trayvon Martin was killed, Obama stated that if he had a son he would look like Trayvon Martin. I think that if Satan had a son he would look, spiritually, exactly like Barack Hussein Obama.

Like the *beast* from Revelation, he comes to us appearing as a Christian, (having the horns of a lamb), but speaks as a dragon, claiming that Jesus Christ is not necessary for salvation (Snyder, 2013), effectively calling Christ a liar. *"Jesus said to him, "I am the way, the truth, and the life. No one comes to the Father except through Me"* (John 14:6)._

Like the *dragon* from Revelation 12, he has launched a war against those who seek to keep the commandments of God and not the dictates of those on the left (Zahn, 2012).

> *"And the dragon was enraged with the woman, and he went to make war with the rest of her offspring, who keep the commandments of God and have the testimony of Jesus Christ"* (Rev. 12:17).

By the Bible's own definition, because he has denied that Jesus Christ is necessary for salvation, he is an *anti-Christ, "and every spirit that does not confess that Jesus Christ has come in the flesh is not of God. And this is the spirit of the Antichrist, which you have heard was coming, and is now already in the world"* (1 John 4:3).

Like the anti-Christ in Revelation chapter 13, he has insulted the God of creation and is relentless in his attacks on the righteous. *"Then he opened his mouth in blasphemy against God, to blaspheme His name, His tabernacle, and those who dwell in heaven. It was granted to him to make war with the saints and to overcome them. And authority was given him over every tribe, tongue, and nation"* (Rev. 13:6–7).

Again, he is like the *horn* from Daniel chapter 25, insulting the God of the Bible, attacking His followers, and seeking to change the times and laws. He has declared on at least three occasions that America is not a Christian nation (Snyder, 2013). He has sought to do away with the country's motto "In God We Trust" (Jessup, 2010). He and his cohorts have ignored our Constitution and our laws while forcing us to adhere to his own will (Slattery and Closter, 2014). *"He shall speak pompous words against the Most High, shall persecute the saints of the Most High, and shall intend to change times and law. Then the saints shall be given into his hand for a time and times and half a time"* (Daniel 7:25).

And like Herod, this president has used his position to attack the church (Snyder, 2013). *"Now about that time Herod the king stretched out his hand to harass some from the church"* (Acts 12:1). He has created policies that require the church to participate in acts that run contrary to our faith. As Psalm 94:20 says, *"Shall the throne of iniquity, which devises evil by law, Have fellowship with You?"*

More than any before him, Obama has shown himself to be an enemy of the cross of Christ, and yet America, and especially we in the black community, adore him. *"For many walk, of whom I have told you often, and now tell you even weeping, that they are the enemies of the cross of Christ: whose end is destruction, whose god is their belly, and whose glory is in their shame—who set their mind on earthly things"* (Phil. 3:18, 19).

BARACK HUSSEIN OBAMA –
ENEMY OF ISRAEL

*"Moreover I will appoint a place for My people Israel, and will
plant them, that they may dwell in a place of their own and
move no more; nor shall the sons of wickedness oppress them
anymore, as previously"*
(1 Chron. 17:9).

Shortly after Obama was elected, Je$$e Jackson predicted that
America's treatment of Israel would change (Taheri, 2008). Not
surprisingly, Jackson was right. When one considers that the
title of one of the books that the president is credited with writing is
Faith of My Fathers and that excerpts from one of his titles reportedly
mention something to the effect that should the political tide
change he would side with the Muslims, his betrayal of Israel is to
be expected.

Obama does not even seem to be trying to disguise his animosity
towards God's chosen people. In a televised speech early in 2014,
Obama seemed to be signaling to the sons of Ishmael that the US
would not aid Israel in the event that it was attacked. "Israel has the
right to defend herself, by herself," he said, seemingly signaling to
the Arab world that as far as he was concerned Israel was on her own.

Then in February of 2014, Obama's Secretary of State, John
Kerry, seemed to suggest that Israel should face economic boycotts
if they refused to capitulate to the demands of Islamic terrorists.

Another of Kerry's speeches seemed to be encouraging violence against the Jewish state if they failed to accept terrorist demands. "Does Israel want a third intifada?" Kerry asked (Torossian, 2014). When the Obama administration banned US airplanes from flying to Israel, many critics, chief among them Ted Cruz, suspected the act was Obama's own attempt at an economic boycott of Israel disguised as a safety measure (Speyer, 2014). *"A worthless person, a wicked man, walks with a perverse mouth; he winks with his eyes, he shuffles his feet, he points with his fingers; perversity is in his heart, he devises evil continually, he sows discord"* (Prov. 6:12–14).

During his first tenure, various reports have stated that Obama had an agreement with the Palestinians to agree to a UN declaration that would declare a Palestinian state with East Jerusalem as its capital (Perry, 2011). I'm sure that Obama would say that his words were taken out of context but, given his animosity towards Israel and his support of all things Islamic, it would be easy to believe such reports. Some would argue that history has shown that it is a dangerous thing for America to betray Israel, and scripture is very specific on how God feels about nations trying to divide the land that He has given to the children of Israel. *"I will also gather all nations, and bring them down to the Valley of Jehoshaphat; And I will enter into judgment with them there On account of My people, my heritage Israel, whom they have scattered among the nations; they have also divided up My land "*(Joel 3:2). Some believe that 9/11, hurricane Katrina and other natural disasters are the direct consequences of America's betrayal of the Jewish State. In the book, *Israel: The Blessing or the Curse*, the authors John McTernan and Bill Koenig document America's treatment of Israel and the resulting consequences in the form of natural disasters.

Despite the evidence of history, our leaders continue to test the patience of the God of Abraham, Isaac, and Jacob. When members of the Bush administration joined the chorus of those who were condemning Israel for being too "heavy handed" in defending her citizens from those who were blowing up their young people, kidnapping and beheading her soldiers, and cutting open her pregnant women, we experienced the terrorist attacks of 9/11. *"The Lord will bring a nation against you from afar, from the end of the earth, as swift as the eagle flies, a nation whose language you will not understand, a nation of fierce countenance, which does not respect the elderly nor show favor to the young"* (Deut. 28:49–50).

"I also will do this to you: I will even appoint terror over you, wasting disease and fever which shall consume the eyes and cause sorrow of heart. And you shall sow your seed in vain, for your enemies shall eat it (Lev. 26:16).

When the Bush administration supported the dismantling of Israeli settlements and the removal of the settlers, we were struck with Hurricane Katrina. *"In the day that you stood on the other side— In the day that strangers carried captive his forces, when foreigners entered his gates and cast lots for Jerusalem—Even you were as one of them* (Obad. 1:11).

Each time the godfather of terror, Yasser Arafat, visited his good friend Bill Clinton to discuss ways to take away the land of the Israelis, the US experienced some type of financial or natural calamity until finally, Clinton became too preoccupied trying to justify his immoral activities with Monica Lewinsky in the White House to partner with Arafat in undermining Israel.

When Bill Clinton had persuaded Israeli Prime Minister Ehud Olmert to give Arafat and the Palestinians almost everything they were seeking, the Palestinians fell silent and then resorted to violence. History has shown that the Palestinians are not interested in peace. *"For they have healed the hurt of the daughter of My people slightly, Saying, 'Peace, peace!' When there is no peace* (Jeremiah 8:11) Safian (2011) reports that the Palestinians have, in fact, turned down Israeli offers of statehood on three occasions. *"They have said, 'Come, and let us cut them off from being a nation, that the name of Israel may be remembered no more'"* (Psalm 83:4).

Despite the evidence of history and the honesty of the terrorist group Hamas, which makes no secret of their intent to see Israel destroyed, however, our leaders continue to pursue the so-called peace process. Hamas leaders have declared that they are not interested in peace, and will only be satisfied with the destruction of Israel (Kredo, 2014). *"Their tongue is an arrow shot out; It speaks deceit; One speaks peaceably to his neighbor with his mouth, but in his heart he lies in wait"* (Jer. 9:8).

The peace process continually asks the Israelis to surrender what little land they have to those who have demonstrated that they will use that land to launch missile and rocket attacks against Israeli cities. As for the terrorists, they are only required to state that the Israelis have a right to exist. Some trade off—land and lives for what thus far has been rhetoric, lies and rockets. *"For they do not speak peace, but they devise deceitful matters Against the quiet ones in the land"* (Psalm 35:20).

In 2011, the president suggested that the Israelis should retreat to their 1967 borders (Bybelezer, 2011). Such an act would reduce Israel to a width of only nine miles. Thank God for Israeli Prime Minister Benjamin Netanhyahu, who made it clear that such a suicidal move was non-negotiable.

Pastor John Hagee likes to remind us that Israel is the only nation that has a deed and title from God, and scripture bears his observations out. *Moreover, I will appoint a place for My people Israel, and will plant them, that they may dwell in a place of their own and move no more; nor shall the sons of wickedness oppress them anymore, as previously"* (2 Sam. 7:10).

America and the nations of the world may abandon Israel, but the God of creation will never abandon her.

> *"Have you not considered what these people have spoken, saying, 'The two families which the Lord has chosen, He has also cast them off'? Thus they have despised My people, as if they should no more be a nation before them. "Thus says the Lord: 'If My covenant is not with day and night, and if I have not appointed the ordinances of heaven and earth, then I will cast away the*

descendants of Jacob and David My servant, so that I will not take any of his descendants to be rulers over the descendants of Abraham, Isaac, and Jacob. For I will cause their captives to return, and will have mercy on them" (Jer. 33:24–26).

Scripture tells us that Satan, the dragon, hates the nation of Israel, represented by the woman, and her descendants, those who have the testimony of Jesus, Christians. Should not mature Christians be aware of the devil's devices and his tools? *"And the dragon was enraged with the woman, and he went to make war with the rest of her offspring, who keep the commandments of God and have the testimony of Jesus Christ"* (Rev. 12:17).

While Obama requires Israel to make many tangible concessions, the only concession he requires of the terrorist government of the Palestinians is to verbally agree to peace. He asks Israel to renounce property rights in Jerusalem, the city of David. He has asked Israel to return to the indefensible borders of 1967. And he has made American support for Israel at the modern-day tower of Babel, the UN, conditional on the Israelis' making concessions to those sworn to Israel's destruction. While requiring absolutely nothing of the Palestinians, Leon Panetta, Obama's Defense Secretary, reminiscent of the late left-wing journalist Helen Thomas, has demanded that the Israeli's "just get to the damned table!" (Gordst, 2011).

After BHO agreed to do nearly everything except build a nuclear bomb for Iran in his nuclear deal, some questioned his intelligence. But I continue to believe that BHO is extremely intelligent and that the Iranian deal is more about a hatred for Israel than it is about curtailing Iran's nuclear ambitions. As is his custom, King BHO benched the American Congress and first sought the approval of the UN (Hattem, 2015). We later learned that the deal on which congress is supposed to approve or disapprove contains elements agreed upon by Iran and the UN that the US congress and the American people will never see (Hohmann, 2015). Far from supporting the Jewish state, the Obama administration has exhibited hostility to her, while counting terrorist groups such as Hamas and the Muslim Brotherhood as legitimate partners in the peace process. For years the nations of the world have been against tiny Israel. Under the Obama administration, the United States seems to have joined them.

BARACK OBAMA - FIRST HOMOSEXUAL PRESIDENT

"[A]nd turning the cities of Sodom and Gomorrah into ashes, condemned them to destruction, making them an example to those who afterward would live ungodly; and delivered righteous Lot, who was oppressed by the filthy conduct of the wicked (for that righteous man, dwelling among them, tormented his righteous soul from day to day by seeing and hearing their lawless deeds)"
(2 Peter 2:6–8)

Because he supposedly knows the words to the national black anthem and possesses a sense of rhythm (he can blow some sax), some half-heartedly perhaps view Bill Clinton as the nation's first black president. Now, if Clinton can be considered the first black president for these empty reasons, none of which have benefitted the black community one iota, then surely Obama can be considered the nation's first homosexual president. Obama's passion for the promotion of the lifestyle that scripture calls "vile" (Judges 19:24), "wicked" (Gen. 19:7), and an "abomination" (Lev. 18:22) has exceeded even that of former Massachusetts Congressman Barney Frank. When it comes to what constitutes a marriage, Obama and the Democrats once again have found it necessary to correct the creator of the universe. *"Shall the one who contends with the Almighty correct Him? He who rebukes God, let him answer it"* (Job 40:2).

Whereas the Scriptures state unequivocally that marriage is the union of a man and woman *"Nevertheless, because of sexual immorality, let each MAN have his own WIFE, and let each WOMAN have her own HUSBAND"* (1 Cor. 7:2 – emphasis mine)—those on the left have claimed that a man can have a husband and a woman can have a wife. Once again this supposed Christian president has deemed himself wiser than the God he claims to serve.

PERVERTING THE MILITARY

*"And He answered and said to them, "Have you not read that
He who made them at the beginning 'made them male and
female,' and said, 'For this reason a man shall leave his f
ather and mother and be joined to his wife, and the two
shall become one flesh"
(Matthew 19:4–5).*

While feigning to evaluate whether or not homosexuals should be allowed to serve openly in the military, Obama was in fact single-minded in his determination to force homosexuality on our military. His actions showed that he was not at all concerned with *whether* homosexuals should be allowed to serve openly, but *when*. Disregarding the wishes of some military officials, the administration proceeded to shove the lifestyle of Sodom and Gomorrah down the throats of our fighting forces, much like he and his fellows shoved healthcare reform down the collective throats of the nation.

While he shuns Christian events such as the National Day of Prayer (Duin, 2009), the president often attends, or sponsors, events meant to drum up support for the lifestyle of Sodom and Gomorrah (LGBT leaders to attend White House reception honoring Pride Month, 2011). Shortly after forcing the lifestyle of Sodom and Gomorrah on the military, Obama could be found taking a victory lap, more likely trolling for votes, at a homosexual rights dinner given by the deceptively named "Human Rights Commission."

And because perversion is never satisfied, the Obama administration attempted to repeal the military's ban on bestiality (Unruh, 2011). For years, sexual deviants have wanted to be rid of laws prohibiting bestiality. Article 125 of the Uniform Code of Military Justice (UCMJ), much like the Bible, makes little distinction between sodomy and bestiality and bans sodomy. With the repeal of "don't ask, don't tell," Article 125 posed a problem for the citizens of Sodom and Gomorrah. Not to be deterred, the Obama administration saw an opportunity to strike a double blow against morality. If not for the attention brought to this promotion of bestiality by People for the Ethical Treatment of Animals (PETA), this perversion may have gone on to become one of those "laws of the land" that liberals so like to protect.

PROMOTING AND SPREADING THE LIFESTYLE OF SODOM AND GOMORRAH WORLDWIDE WITH OUR TAX DOLLARS

"As Sodom and Gomorrah, and the cities around them in a similar manner to these, having given themselves over to sexual immorality and gone after strange flesh, are set forth as an example, suffering the vengeance of eternal fire. Likewise also these dreamers defile the flesh, reject authority, and speak evil of dignitaries
(Jude 1:7–8).

Demonstrating that perversion is never satisfied, Obama recently made the promotion of the lifestyle of Sodom and Gomorrah a matter of foreign policy. The Obama administration has announced that it will tie any US foreign aid to the promotion of the lifestyle of Sodom and Gomorrah (US to use foreign aid to promote gay rights, 2011). He has directed US government agencies to use taxpayer dollars to promote the spread of the lifestyle of Sodom and Gomorrah and to withhold US aid from those nations that refuse to embrace the lifestyle that the creator calls abominable. Obama having won election and reelection, put aside the facade that he believes marriage is the union of a man and a woman.

His apparent inconsistency on the topic of marriage (Ford, 2011) was all for political expediency. His announcement that he supports the state-sanctioned promotion of the lifestyle of Sodom and Gomorrah (Calmes and Baker, 2012) came as big news to some, though it shouldn't have. Even before he was elected, Obama declared that if elected he would use the position of the presidency to spread the lifestyle of Sodom and Gomorrah. He also said that he would seek to completely repeal the Defense of Marriage Act (DOMA).

His appointees, his elimination of "don't ask, don't tell," his refusal to defend the DOMA laws, and his speeches at pro-homosexual events all lead one to believe that Obama is exactly who Larry Sinclair, the man who claimed to have had a homosexual relationship with Obama, says Obama is (Corsi, 2012). And this supposed "evolution" on what constitutes a marriage is no evolution at all.

Whether Obama's announcement was a result of political calculation, or whether he was forced into it by Vice President Biden's announced support of the lifestyle of Sodom and Gomorrah (Altman, 2012), those with eyes to see and ears to hear recognize that Obama's support of this lifestyle has been ever present. Why else would he call for an end to the DOMA?

And as I read the reports of black Christian pastors' reactions to BHO's announcement that he now supports what he calls same-sex marriage, I was saddened, but not surprised, to see that given the choice between Christ and political affiliation, political affiliation once again wins. Many said that although they disagreed with Obama they would still support him; others agreed with him completely; and only a few said that they could not support one who held such a position.

Demonstrating who they really serve, black church leaders met to find a way to "inspire" blacks to continue in their support of Obama (Walsten, 2012), and not the precepts of God. They needn't have put forth any effort as, unfortunately, we in the black community are much more obedient to the dictates of the Democrats than we are to the word of God. When we who profess Christ put the policies of a political party ahead of the words of God, it is no longer God that we serve but that political party. Surely, such a person's religion is in vain. *"And in vain they worship Me, Teaching as doctrines the commandments of men.' For laying aside the commandment of God, you hold the tradition of men —the washing of pitchers and cups, and many other such things you do." He said to them, "All too well you reject the commandment of God, that you may keep your tradition.* (Mark 7:7–9). It didn't take long for our so-called black leaders to come out in support of Obama's announcement. Jackson, Sharpton, the NAACP, and others joined Obama in condemning the biblical definition of marriage (Reynolds, 2012). *"Would you indeed annul My judgment? Would you condemn Me that you may be justified?* (Job 40:8).

As is always the case with those on the left, even those who give lip service to Christianity, they do not hesitate to instruct the God of creation when his precepts are contrary to their love of darkness. *"Shall the one who contends with the Almighty correct Him? He who rebukes God, let him answer it"* (Job 40:2).

The citizens of Sodom and Gomorrah have been gaining ground in the US. Not satisfied that they are free to engage in acts that scripture calls wicked, unnatural, and abominable, they insist that all of the nation accept and celebrate those acts. *"Do not prattle," you say to those who prophesy. So they shall not prophesy to you; they shall not return insult for insult* (Micah 2:6). And they are laying the groundwork to make opposition to those acts a punishable crime. Today we fight for the God-ordained institution of marriage. If decency and morality fail, the next battle will be for the protection of our children, as even now some of those on the left have begun to seek the acceptance of pedophilia, under the pseudonyms "trans-generational or inter-generational sex."

Representatives from some of Americans most influential organizations, including Johns Hopkins, the American Psychiatric Association (APA) and Harvard, met in 2011 to discuss ways to gain sympathy for, and present pedophiles in a positive light

(Brown, 2011). This attempt at normalizing pedophilia along with the Obama administration's characterization of children as "sexual beings" (Ertelt, 2011) demonstrates the left's unspoken creed of "laying hands on their little ones."

So, if Clinton can be considered the nation's first black president, Obama certainly should be considered the nation's first homosexual president, figuratively speaking, and according to some reports and a Mr. Larry Sinclair, perhaps literally as well. Even members of the Taliban suspect that BHO is a homosexual (Fitzgerald, 2015). Nationwide, homosexuals are becoming more powerful. Many God-fearing people have lost their jobs or been harshly criticized for simply stating or defending their belief in the God-ordained institution of marriage (Beale, 2013). *"Nevertheless, because of sexual immorality, let each man have his own wife, and let each woman have her own husband"* (1 Cor. 7:2).

Those who promote and practice that very lifestyle practiced by the citizens of Sodom and Gomorrah like to paint any opposition to it as intolerance. When it comes to homosexuality, Christians aren't tolerated. Homosexual acceptance has become BHO's golden idol. Just as Nebuchadnezzar punished those who would not bow down to his golden statue, so is America punishing those who refuse to celebrate and promote the lifestyle of Sodom and Gomorrah.

Among those I have known who lived the homosexual lifestyle were three young men. All three are currently in the grave, a direct result of practicing this "alternative lifestyle." One never reached the age of 30, dying in his early 20s; another never reached 40, dying in his late 30s; and the fourth didn't make it to 50, dying in his late 40s.

BARACK HUSSEIN OBAMA –
MOST SUCCESSFUL PRESIDENT

*Rest in the Lord, and wait patiently for Him; Do not fret
because of him who prospers in his way, Because of the man
who brings wicked schemes to pass
(Ps. 37:7).*

Just as fools are not necessarily stupid, I think it may be fair to say that this worst president in the history of our nation has also been one of the most successful presidents in the nation's history. Many of BHO's critics and opponents think that he, BHO, is incompetent, in over his head and has thus far had a failed presidency. However, I see it as being completely the opposite. I see a brilliant, though evil, president who knows exactly what he is doing. I see the most successful president in recent memory, when one considers that he has succeeded in accomplishing most of the objectives he set out to achieve. In 2008, then Senator Obama declared that he wanted to fundamentally change America (Hanson, 2013).

During nearly eight years as president, BHO has definitely changed America, and not for the better. Again in 2008, BHO declared that if elected president he would use the office to overturn the biblical definition of marriage, in favor of state sanctioned unions that mimicked the lifestyle practiced by the citizens of Sodom and Gomorrah (Winn, 2008). And in June of 2015, activist, tyrannical, supreme court justices, one of them an Obama appointee suspected of being a homosexual herself, decided that democracy had no place concerning the issue, that they would impose their wills on the millions of Americans who viewed marriage as the union of male and female, in favor of the few who wanted the lifestyle of Sodom and Gomorrah to be an unquestionable and celebrated right (Resnick, Fox & Volz, 2015).

Supporting the administration's crusade for transforming America into a modern day version of Sodom and Gomorrah, Robert Gates, president of the Boy Scouts of America (BSA), has deemed that the BSA's ban on homosexual leaders will come to an end (Eckholm, 2015). What the Catholic church took away from homosexual pedophiles, Gates has returned to them; authority over impressionable, powerless, young boys. Obama's desire to redistribute America's wealth was well known and he has been successful at doing just that through lies, manipulations, and subterfuge in the form of the Affordable Care Act (ACA).

The ACA was passed through backroom deals, bribery and outright lies (Pruitt, 2015), the most famous of which was BHO's blatant lie that people would be able to keep their current health care plans and doctors if they wanted to. Not even the videotaped admissions of ACA architect Jonathan Gruber boasting of the underhanded methods used to sell Obamacare and of relying on the "stupidity" of American voters for its passage (Fitzgerald, 2015), or challenges to the plain wording of a portion of the law that concerned subsidies (Foxnews.com, 2015) were enough to convince a tyrannical supreme court that this law was passed through fraudulent means and should be repealed or revisited with input from the opposing Republican party, all of whom opposed its passage.

Aided for the second time by Obamacare's greatest ally, Chief Justice John Roberts, the supreme court took it upon themselves to disregard the wording of the law (Liptak, 2015) and instead, as has become the habit of many of the nation's judges resorted to tyranny rather than justice, and to enforce their will upon what used to be a democratic nation. "How strangely will the Tools of a Tyrant pervert the plain Meaning of Words!" – Samuel Adams (Goodreads.com, 2015). Exhibiting a disdain for America, second only to his seeming hatred for Israel, BHO has embraced our enemies and persecuted our friends. In moves that are more capitulation than negotiation he has let jihadist dictate the terms for the release of deserter sergeant Beau Bergdahl; in keeping with his never ending criticism of America, he has joined Cuba's Fidel Castro in insulting America (Noble, 2013).

In a move that I believe lays the ground for an excuse for closing Guantanamo prison, BHO has resumed normal relations with Cuba. In another move that I believe has more to do with a supernatural hatred of Israel than securing BHO's legacy or curtailing Iran's nuclear ambitions, BHO held what appeared to be never ending negotiations (capitulation), extending the deadline numerous times with Iran. After having dictated the terms of the deal, the Iranian leaders celebrated by attending a death to America rally (Lieberman, 2015).

BHO's latest capitulation and betrayal of our friends involves an agreement in which Turkey will finally, after previously denying us, allow the US to use their air bases in the fight against BHO's true legacy, ISIS. In exchange Turkey gets to kill the Kurds, the one group that has been successfully battling ISIS (Cole, 2015). America, as I see it, becomes an accomplice to the murder of every Kurdistan fighter killed by Turkey; yet another act of treachery against our friends. This administration has shown bravery in combating Israelis, the biblical definition of marriage, Christians, their natural enemies, the unborn, the Washington Redskins football team, and now the Kurds, but when it comes to Iran, Cuba, Russia, and ISIS, there is only capitulation, pacification, and empty words. Under BHO, our Constitution has become null and void as he continues to ignore it. Our congress seems to be useless as BHO has consulted with the Arab League and the UN for advice, while casting our congress and our constitution aside. In 2001, then Senator Obama expressed his belief that we needed to "break free" of constitutional constraints (Gregory, 2012); as president he has done exactly that.

I do not question BHO's intelligence but that of those who fail to see what he's been doing. He has ignored the laws that he swore to uphold. Using accusations of racism as a battering ram he has nullified those who should have held him accountable. Aided by his greatest ally, the mainstream media, he is able to use half- truths, omissions and outright lies to gain the support of society. With words alone he has kept a fearful and spineless opposition party from honoring our system of checks and balances. The Middle Eastern terrorists haven't been able to change our way of life, but the terrorist sympathizer in the white House has succeeded in doing just that.

CHAPTER 5

WHO IS ON THE LORD'S SIDE

*And Elijah came to all the people, and said, "How long will you falter between **two opinions**? If the Lord is God, follow Him; but if Baal, follow him." But the people answered him not a word-* (1 Kings 18:21)

MEDIA

They have grown fat, they are sleek; Yes, they surpass the deeds
of the wicked; They do not plead the cause, the cause of the
fatherless; Yet they prosper, And the right of the
needy they do not defend
(Jer. 5:28).

While the black community may be the Democrats' most loyal supporters, it is a biased media that are their most effective supporters. They fail to report anything that may cast liberal Democrats in a negative light. Yet, they have even stooped to fabricating stories to discredit or call into question the integrity of evangelicals and conservatives.

In what I believe is a blatant display of media bias, CNN, sometimes called the "Clinton News Network," sought to derail Dr. Ben Carson's political aspirations by attempting to portray him as a liar. CNN has called into question the life story of Dr. Carson, questioning the validity of events that happened over fifty years ago.[29] They have chosen to focus on Dr. Carson's decades old past while Hillary Clinton's very recent scandals and proven lies have been ignored.

They do not care that the woman who would be president has admitted to lying about the Benghazi attack,[30] or that she broke the law by using a private email server while serving as secretary of state.[31] The long and questionable records of both Clintons goes back for years, even before Bill was president, and the media continues to give them a pass. Few have heard of the scandal called "Blood Gate" in which Bill Clinton, while governor of Arkansas, was implicated in a scheme that sold hepatitis- and HIV-tainted blood to unsuspecting patients, resulting in the deaths of at least 3,000 and the infection of at least 1,000 people.[32]

The media ignores what appear to be the Clinton's years-long habit of selling America's security and secrets for profit and power. They did not question why Hillary Clinton approved a transaction that gave Vladimir Putin the rights to one-fifth of America's uranium, or the subsequent flow of millions in donations to the Clinton Foundation[33]. The selling out of America is not new to the Clintons. During Bill Clinton's time in office, donations from the Chinese military to the Democrat Party resulted in China gaining sensitive American missile technology[34]. Aside from using this technology for its own military, some suspect that it's also responsible for the success of the North Korean missile program[35]. Thank you, Bill Clinton.

Of course, these incidents pale in comparison as to whether Dr. Carson's actions of over fifty years ago are true or not. Normal rules do not apply to the Clintons. Hillary had no reservations about finding a reason to arrest the video maker that she blamed for the terror attacks at Benghazi. She has condemned Edward Snowden for putting America's security at risk [1116] while ignoring her recent actions. During the first democratic presidential debate she declared that every child should have the opportunity to live up to his or her God given potential, yet she defends the murder of unborn and newly born children.

After ISIS sympathizer, and suspected homosexual, Omar Mateen slaughtered forty-nine innocents at an Orlando gay bar, I waited to see if the mass hypnotists, as they usually do, would find some way to blame the tragedy on Christians, conservatives, and Republicans. Liberals, for all of their supposed intelligence, have a hard time making the distinction between disagreement and hate. And while they are very good at blaming Christians, conservatives, and Republicans for every negative thing that involves homosexuals, even homosexual suicides, their righteous indignation dissipates when it comes to Muslims. For example, in his interview of, Florida Attorney General, Pam Bondi CNN's Anderson Cooper seemed to insinuate that opposition to "gay marriage" could encourage people to physically attack homosexuals (Richter, 2016).

Instead of placing the entire blame where it belonged, on confirmed Islamic terrorist, suspected homosexual, and registered Democrat, Omar Mateen, Mr. Cooper had to find a way to partially blame those who believe in the biblical definition of marriage. If we truly hated homosexuals, as liberals like to pretend, then we would join them in promoting it. I've witnessed the depression, despair, and death that homosexuality has led to in the lives of some wonderful people. If we truly hated homosexuals, then we'd join BHO and those on the left hand in their calls to bring hundreds of thousands of Muslim immigrants to our nation. We know how Muslims feel about homosexuality.

After the slaughter in Orlando, BHO contended that Americans needed to change their attitudes about homosexuals (Podhoretz, 2016). Will he lecture the hundreds of thousands of Muslims that he seeks to import about their attitudes towards homosexuals as well? The media, and those on the left, would have us practice Christianity according to their guidelines, not Christ's. They have used homosexuality to attack Christians much like Nebuchadnezzar's governors used the golden idol to attack Daniel (Dan. 6:4–9). You either bow down and pay homage to it, or you suffer the consequences. Whether it is child murder (Isa. 13:18), dictating how Christians should practice their faith (Acts 4:17–19) or promoting deviant sexual behavior (Gen. 19: 4–5) Satan has no new tricks; he only repackages them, and his servants are only too happy to carry them out. While the media searches high and low for instances of Christians persecuting homosexuals, they turn a blind eye to the religious persecution that Christians face for simply adhering to their faith. *"They have grown fat, they are sleek; yes, they surpass the deeds of the wicked; They do not plead the cause, the cause of the fatherless; Yet they prosper, And the right of the needy they do not defend* (Jer. 5:28). When Christians are fired for merely stating a belief in biblical marriage (Marie, 2014), face ridiculous lawsuits, protests, boycotts, and even receive death threats (Beale, 2013) this is news that the media doesn't deem worthy of any significant print. For those who have wondered aloud about how two men marrying will hurt anyone, the above is but a small sampling of how it has already hurt many Christians, life-changing, extremely negative, consequences for merely stating a belief in the God-ordained, biblical definition of marriage. I strongly believe that homosexuals should not be harassed because of their sexual preferences, but neither should Christians be persecuted because of their faith.

BLACK CHURCH:
CONFESSING CHRIST, SUPPORTING SATAN?

"I marvel that you are turning away so soon from Him who called you in the grace of Christ, to a different gospel, which is not another; but there are some who trouble you and want to pervert the gospel of Christ. But even if we, or an angel from heaven, preach any other gospel to you than what we have preached to you, let him be accursed"
(Gal. 1:6–8).

And then there's the black church, the moral compass of the people. During the period of slavery, slave masters sought to use verses of scripture to help ensure the subservience of the slaves. But the slaves instead took inspiration from the word of God. They recognized that just as the God of Abraham, Isaac, and Jacob had eventually freed the Jews from the bondage of the Egyptians, so too would he also free them from the brutality of slavery in America. And well after the end of slavery it was ministers who were at the forefront of the fight for equal rights for blacks. The most notable, of course, was the Reverend Martin Luther King Jr. Today, Dr. King's niece, Dr. Alveda King, carries on his legacy by trying to free blacks from a different kind of slavery, that of social and mental enslavement.

As for the black ministers of today, they should be exposing the damage being done to the black community by so-called black leaders and the Democrat Party. But one must search far and wide to find black pastors whose allegiance is to Christ and not to political affiliation. Among those who profess Christ, only the black churches support the party dedicated to outlawing Christ, through so-called hate crimes and hate speech laws. Only the black churches, without question, support a party dedicated to murdering unborn babies, and that not only remain silent in their approval of those dedicated to spreading the lifestyle of Sodom and Gomorrah nationwide but also cast their support behind those who have made no secret of their plans to spread that lifestyle. It is so frustrating to watch as the black clergy sit silently as homosexuals compare their choice of a lifestyle to being born black.

For most of their lives many in the black church will profess Christ, but every two years when election season rolls around, we cast aside the commandments of God in favor of the commandments of the Democrat Party.

> *Therefore the Lord said: "Inasmuch as these people draw near with their mouths And honor Me with their lips, But have removed their hearts far from Me, And their fear toward Me is taught by the commandment of men, therefore, behold, I will again do a marvelous work Among this people, A marvelous work and a wonder; tor the wisdom of their wise men shall perish, And the understanding of their prudent men shall be hidden"* (Isa. 29:13–14).

While Christ commands that we love the Lord our God with all our hearts, souls, and minds, the Democrats say that all faiths are equal, and through their surrogates have outlawed prayer in our schools and outlawed even the mention of Jesus' name in public. As it says in Acts 4:18, *"So they called them and commanded them not to speak at all nor teach in the name of Jesus."*

The Word of God is clear concerning the practice of homosexuality. The Bible calls that lifestyle wicked, vile, unnatural, and abominable. The Democrat party, however, calls it a safe, natural alternative lifestyle and is constantly seeking to punish any who would dare to say otherwise.

The Word of God warns us against shedding innocent blood, commands us to defend those who can't defend themselves, and declares that children are gifts from God. The Democrat party begs to differ. Barack Obama, in his wisdom, has overridden God's authority. Far from being the gifts that God, apparently *mistakenly*, believes they are according to Psalm 127:3, *"Behold, children are a heritage from the Lord, the fruit of the womb is a reward* Mr. Obama has decreed that babies are in fact a form of punishment (Baggot, 2008). On several occasions while serving as a senator in Illinois, Obama opposed legislation that would have provided medical care to newborns who had survived an attempted murder (Stanek, 2008). Even after a federal law was passed that prevented this murderous act, which was considered by many to be nothing short of infanticide, Obama was resistant to providing care for newborns who survived abortions.

Even Barbara Boxer and NARAL, the most ardent supporters of murdering unborn babies, supported the act. But Obama alone opposed, and prevented the act from passing. It would not be until 2005 when Obama was no longer in the Illinois Senate that the act would pass. Some reports say that Obama personally blocked the acts passage on at least four occasions. As we have seen throughout Obama's presidency, few things are as striking as his and his party's covenant with death. On more than one occasion they have demonstrated a willingness to withhold military funding and to shut down the entire government if funding to those in the business of slaughtering unborn babies was denied. *"Because you have said, 'We have made a covenant with death, and with Sheol we are in agreement. When the overflowing scourge passes through, it will not come to us, for we have made lies our refuge, and under falsehood we have hidden ourselves"* (Isa. 28:15).

And so for a time Obama, like a certain figure in Hebrews 2:14, held the power of death. We may never know how many babies died simply because this one individual refused to allow them medical care.

The fruits of the Democrat Party are the criminalization of Christ, the spread of the lifestyle of Sodom and Gomorrah, and multiple millions of murdered unborn babies. So when given the chance to abide in the doctrine of Christ or support the Democrat Party, 90 percent of the black community will support anti-Christs, sexual deviants, and child murderers. And let's not deceive ourselves, if those who support, encourage, and defend the murder of unborn babies are not murderers then neither was Pharaoh, Herod, or Hitler. Neither of these evil men personally murdered the great numbers of people that they are credited with murdering, but through their policies and authority millions were murdered.

And what should be frightening to the black community, especially those who claim Christ, is that scripture suggests that in the eyes of God we who support such people are just as guilty of their crimes as if we had committed them ourselves. *"Whoever transgresses and does not abide in the doctrine of Christ does not have God. He who abides in the doctrine of Christ has both the Father and the Son. If anyone comes to you and does not bring this doctrine, do not receive him into your house nor greet him; for he who greets him shares in his evil deeds"* (2 John 1:9–11).

And, again, Scripture suggests that we will indeed receive the same reward as those we support. If we support and empower the righteous, we will receive the same reward as they, and if we support and empower the wicked, we can expect to receive the same reward they receive.

> *"He who receives a prophet in the name of a prophet shall receive a prophet's reward. And he who receives a righteous man in the name of a righteous man shall receive a righteous man's reward"* (Matt. 10:41).

PASTORS

"Preach the word! Be ready in season and out of season.
Convince, rebuke, exhort, with all longsuffering and teaching.
For the time will come when they will not endure sound
doctrine, but according to their own desires, because they have
itching ears, they will heap up for themselves teachers; and they
will turn their ears away from the truth, and be turned
aside to fables"
(2 Timothy 4:2–4).

It is no surprise that black leaders and politicians have sold the black community to the *Demon*cratic Party. In his letter from a Birmingham jail, Martin Luther King Jr. stated that racial divisions would be profitable for some in the black community. I'm often critical of the Republican Party for putting the party over principle. But many black pastors have proven that when it comes to choosing the precepts of Christ over the dictates of the Democrat party, the Democrats win hands down. Many of our pastors feign allegiance to Christ until the political seasons roll around, and then their actions and their words reveal who it is that they truly serve. For those who profess Christ scripture should be relevant at all times including the political season.

Rather than reproving the enemies of Christ, rather than rebuking those who advocate for the murder of unborn babies, rather than exhorting the people to execute righteous judgment in their choice of leaders, most of our pastors will encourage their followers to support those things that God condemns. *"You shall not lie with a male as with a woman. It is an abomination"* (Lev. 18:22). Ignoring character and setting aside the Word of God during the political season, our pastors will endorse individuals who make the Pharisees and Sadducees of Jesus' time seem righteous. *"Moreover thou shalt provide out of all the people able men, such as fear God, men of truth, hating covetousness: and place such over them, to be rulers of thousands, and rulers of hundreds, rulers of fifties, and rulers of tens"* (Ex. 18:21).

During the 2008 presidential campaign, some black pastors chose to criticize those who were opposed to Obama's dedication to the murder of unborn babies and his belief that Jesus Christ is not necessary for salvation. *"Jesus said to him, "I am the way, the truth, and the life. No one comes to the Father except through Me"* (John 14:6). Instead of contending for Christ, these pastors chose to run to the defense of one who has consistently denied Christ and Christianity (Marcus, 2012). How unseemly for Christian pastors to ignore the laws of God and heap praise upon one who has demonstrated nothing but hostility to Christianity. *"Those who forsake the law praise the wicked, but such as keep the law contend with them"* (Prov. 28:4).

One prominent televangelist, pastor of a megachurch, sounding much like Hillary Clinton when she claimed that those opposed to the murder of unborn babies and those who promote it could find common ground, claimed that he would like to see black and white Christians find common ground. This pastor declared that a victory for Obama would be a victory for African Americans and democracy. The sad truth is that Obama scored a victory for Antichrists, for those in the business of murdering unborn and newly born children, for those who practice the lifestyle of Sodom and Gomorrah and for radical Islamists worldwide.

And there is **no** common ground between life and death, light and darkness, good and evil. *"Do not be unequally yoked together with unbelievers. For what fellowship has righteousness with lawlessness? And what communion has light with darkness"* (2 Cor. 6:14)?

Other black pastors were offended by some who characterized Obama as an anti-Christ (Meyer, 2008). While Obama may not be ***the*** Antichrist, by scripture's own definition, he definitely is ***an*** antichrist. *For many deceivers have gone out into the world who do not confess Jesus Christ as coming in the flesh. This is a deceiver and an antichrist"* (2 John 1:7).

Still other black pastors took it upon themselves to defend Obama's Christianity—a Christianity that denies Christ, mocks the Bible, and elevates Islam (70 Pastors Got It Wrong … I Got It Right, 2010). *"Most assuredly, I say to you, he who does not enter the sheepfold by the door, but climbs up some other way, the same is a thief and a robber"* (John 10:1). These pastors, who I hope believe in free speech, took it upon themselves to tell others what they could and could not say or even think. It is very disappointing that after years of studying and preaching God's word, these pastors are unable to distinguish between good and evil.

> *For though by this time you ought to be teachers, you need someone to teach you again the first principles of the oracles of God; and you have come to need milk and not solid food. For everyone who partakes only of milk is unskilled in the word of righteousness, for he is a babe. But solid food belongs to those who are of full age, that is, those who by reason of use have their senses exercised to discern both good and evil"* (Hebrews 5:12–14).

Should not our pastors be protecting the sheep instead of hand delivering them to the wolves?

> *The thief does not come except to steal, and to kill, and to destroy. I have come that they may have life, and that they may have it more abundantly. I am the good shepherd. The good shepherd gives His life for the sheep. But a hireling, he who is not the shepherd, one who does not own the sheep, sees the wolf coming and leaves the sheep and flees; and the wolf catches the sheep and scatters them. The hireling flees because he is a hireling and does*

not care about the sheep. I am the good shepherd; and I know
My sheep, and am known by My own (John 10:10–14).

How patient is our God that he has endured this bitter betrayal
by the black community? For years now we have empowered the
Democrat Party. A party that never ceases in its attempts at outlawing
Christ. *"They set up kings, but not by Me; They made princes, but I did*
not acknowledge them. From their silver and gold they made idols for
themselves—that they might be cut off" (Hosea 8:4).

Will we reject Scripture's definitions of good and evil, will
we support the enemies of the cross of Christ, advocates for child
murder and promoters of deviant sexual behavior. Will we teach our
children that those who are hostile to Christ are "good"? *You have*
wearied the Lord with your words; Yet you say, "In what way have we
wearied Him?" In that you say, "Everyone who does evil Is good in the
sight of the Lord, And He delights in them," Or, "Where is the God of
justice?" (Mal. 2:17)._

Scripture tells us that God considers it a horrible deed when
those who profess to serve him are in the business of empowering the
wicked. *"Also I have seen a horrible thing in the prophets of Jerusalem:*
They commit adultery and walk in lies; they also strengthen the hands
of evildoers, so that no one turns back from his wickedness. all of them
are like Sodom to Me, And her inhabitants like Gomorrah (Jer. 23: 14).

Come election season many of our pastors will invoke the civil
rights movement in urging us to turn out and support those on the
left hand. They will mention the amount of blood that was shed by
blacks just so that we might have the right to vote. But none will
mention that our votes have been, and are being, used to shed the
blood of millions and millions of innocent unborn babies, both black
and white. Al Sharpton, in urging blacks to turn out and strengthen
the hands of those who are contrary to everything that is Christ,
stated, "Go to the polls Tuesday in the name of our ancestors. Know
that yours is a bloodstained ballot. This is a sacred obligation."

But, this pastor was right on one point. Ours is indeed a blood
stained ballot. Ever since we cast our lot with those on the left hand

we have used our ballots to spill the blood of millions and millions of unborn babies, the greater percentage of them blacks. *"My son, if sinners entice you, do not consent. If they say, "Come with us, Let us lie in wait to shed blood; Let us lurk secretly for the innocent without cause; let us swallow them alive like Sheol, and whole, like those who go down to the Pit; we shall find all kinds of precious possessions, we shall fill our houses with spoil; Cast in your lot among us, Let us all have one purse"—My son, do not walk in the way with them, Keep your foot from their path; For their feet run to evil, And they make haste to shed blood* (Prov. 1:10–16).

As I listen to and read the words of some of these black pastors I cannot help but to think that it is the Democrat Party and not the God of Abraham, Isaac, and Jacob that they worship. With the apostle Paul I say, *"I marvel that you are turning away so soon from Him who called you in the grace of Christ, to a different gospel, which is not another; but there are some who trouble you and want to pervert the gospel of Christ. But even if we, or an angel from heaven, preach any other gospel to you than what we have preached to you, let him be accursed* (Galatians 1: 6–8).

And in a move that perfectly demonstrates what I like to call confessing Christ and supporting Satan, in 2012 several hundred black pastors took the advice of the corrupt Eric Holder, the anti-Christian ACLU, and the IRS, silencer of conservative churches, on how to best participate in the 2012 election (Gehrke, 2012). And if Christ's sheep hear Christ's voice, (John 10: 4, 5) to whom do these pastors belong that hearken to the advice of antichrists, advocates for child murder, and promoters of the homosexual lifestyle?

Are they even sheep at all? *All the nations will be gathered before Him, and He will separate them one from another, as a shepherd divides his sheep from the goats. And He will set the sheep on His right hand, but the goats on the left* (Matt. 25:32, 33).

Will we continue to reject the commands of Christ in favor of political affiliation, and then without shame come before him on

Sundays to feign obedience. Jeremiah 7:8–10 accuses, *"Behold, you trust in lying words that cannot profit. Will you steal, murder, commit adultery, swear falsely, burn incense to Baal, and walk after other gods whom you do not know, and then come and stand before Me in this house which is called by My name, and say, 'We are delivered to do all these abominations'?*

Each day brings us closer to the coming of Christ. No amount of church attendance, prayers, Bible studies, or empty words of repentance will gain murderers, or those that support murderers, entry into the Kingdom of God. In fact, scripture tells us that God hates the pretense of those who have taken his name in vain but live contrary to his precepts.

> *Bring no more futile sacrifices; incense is an abomination to me. The new moons, the Sabbaths, and the calling of assemblies I cannot endure iniquity and the sacred meeting. Your new Moons and your appointed feasts my soul hates; they are a trouble to Me, I am weary of bearing them. When you spread out your hands, I will hide my eyes from you; even though you make many prayers I will not hear. Your hands are full of blood. Wash yourselves, make yourselves clean; put away the evil of your doings from before My eyes. Cease to do evil. Learn to do good; seek justice, rebuke the oppressor; defend the fatherless, plead for the widow. Bring no more futile sacrifices; Incense is an abomination to Me. The New Moons, the Sabbaths, and the calling of assemblies—I cannot endure iniquity and the sacred meeting. Your New Moons and your appointed feasts My soul hates; They are a trouble to Me, I am weary of bearing them. When you spread out your hands, I will hide My eyes from you; Even though you make many prayers, I will not hear. Your hands are full of blood. Wash yourselves, make yourselves clean; put away the evil of your doings from before My eyes. Cease to do evil, learn to do good; Seek justice, Rebuke the oppressor; Defend the fatherless, Plead for the widow* (Isa. 1:13, 15–17).

We place ourselves and, by our example, our young in danger of the judgment when we continue to claim Christ, yet are obedient to a political party. Matthew 7:21–23 reads as though it was written specifically for the church. God is not satisfied with lip service and a lukewarm lifestyle. He demands obedience. *"Not everyone who says to Me, 'Lord, Lord,' shall enter the kingdom of heaven, but he who does the will of My Father in heaven. Many will say to Me in that day, 'Lord, Lord, have we not prophesied in Your name, cast out demons in Your name, and done many wonders in Your name?' And then I will declare to them, 'I never knew you; depart from Me, you who practice lawlessness"* (Matt. 7:21–23)!

The above passage should spur all who claim Christ to take inventory of their lives (as in 2 Cor. 13:5).

Christians, even in our imperfections, should be contending for the faith of Christ not strengthening the hands of those, democrats, who are constantly seeking ways to outlaw the faith. In his epistle, Jude exhorts Christians in verse 3, *"Beloved, while I was very diligent to write to you concerning our common salvation, I found it necessary to write to you exhorting you to contend earnestly for the faith which was once for all delivered to the saints.*

Under the leadership of those on the left hand, and especially this current White House, America has begun to resemble the nation spoken of in Revelation 18:2, *"And he cried mightily with a loud voice, saying, 'Babylon the great is fallen, is fallen, and has become a dwelling place of demons, a prison for every foul spirit, and a cage for every unclean and hated bird!'"*

The moral degradation that is the American society, and those individuals who are leading it should distress those who follow Christ as much as the actions of Sodom and Gomorrah's inhabitants distressed righteous Lot. *"for that righteous man, dwelling among them, tormented his righteous soul from day to day by seeing and hearing their lawless deeds) (2 Peter 2:8).*

Like the men of Jerusalem in Ezekiel 9:4, Christians should be saddened by America's transformation into a nation that greatly resembles the Babylon of Revelation 18:2. Today, under the influence of those on the left hand, and thanks to a complicit church, America, as someone recently stated, is no longer great or good. As we have tossed aside the values that made us a great nation we have lost the respect of the world. In their speeches our leaders boldly proclaim "God Bless America" then they set out to erase God from society.

One of the most telling signs that we are, perhaps, no longer under the blessings of God is that we are now a nation of borrowers, becoming the servants of the lenders. Chapter 28 of the book of Deuteronomy describes both the nation that is blessed by God and the nation that is cursed by God. When it comes to blessing and curses, America's leaders continue to choose the curses.

> *"Behold, I set before you today a blessing and a curse: the blessing, if you obey the commandments of the Lord your God which I command you today; and the curse, if you do not obey the commandments of the Lord your God, but turn aside from the way which I command you today, to go after other gods which you have not known– (Deut. 11:26–28).*

And like the apostles of Acts, we should boldly proclaim that we will follow God, not political affiliation. *"But Peter and the other apostles answered and said: "We ought to obey God rather than men* (Acts 5:29).

ENEMIES OF CHRIST

*"For many walk, of whom I have told you often, and now
tell you even weeping, that they are the enemies of the cross of
Christ: whose end is destruction, whose god is their belly, and
whose glory is in their shame—who set their mind on
earthly things
(Phil. 3:18–19).*

The first politician who thought that he knew better than the God
of creation was Lucifer. His campaign to replace God gained
him the support of one-third of the angels of heaven. Today
his children, those on the left, liberals like their father, would also
claim to know better than God. *"You are of your father the devil, and
the desires of your father you want to do. He was a murderer from the
beginning, and does not stand in the truth, because there is no truth
in him. When he speaks a lie, he speaks from his own resources, for he
is a liar and the father of it* (John 8:44)._God has recognized the
value of the lives of the unborn, but liberal Democrats say God is
wrong. God ordained the institution of marriage between a man and
a woman and condemned the life style practiced by the citizens of
Sodom and Gomorrah, again liberal Democrats reject the creator's
view and if possible would jail all those who disagree.

On more than one occasion BHO has found it necessary to
declare to the world that the US is no longer a Christian nation.
This contention is one of the few things on which I agree with
BHO. Under the influence of those on the left hand, America bears

little resemblance to a Christian nation. No Christian nation would enshrine into law the same acts committed by the cities of Sodom and Gomorrah. Would a Christian nation follow the examples of Herod, Pharaoh and the great red dragon of revelation and murder the most vulnerable of its population, children? It seems unthinkable that a Christian nation would make the mere mention of Jesus' name in public a crime. A recent Pew Research Survey found that even though Christianity in American has declined, 70.6 percent of the population still consider themselves Christians (Naylor, 2015). Many would find BHO's statement concerning America and Christianity offensive and statistics would seem to disprove it but when one considers the things that America holds dear, the legal ability to murder unborn children and the promotion of the life style practiced by the residents of Sodom and Gomorrah, and the fact that merely mentioning Jesus name in public is a significant offense, it becomes clear that America is decidedly anti- Christian.

While it appears that the number of Christians has declined, the Pew Survey found that those who consider themselves evangelicals, or born again, have remained stable (Zylstra, 2015). In today's America, Christianity is increasingly portrayed as an offensive and divisive religion. Some on the left, including BHO, have even taken to equating peaceful Christians with violent Islamic terrorists. Many well- meaning people have rejected religion outright and taken to describing themselves as being spiritual instead of religious. After reading the results of the Pew Research poll my mind immediately turned to the parable of the sower from Matthew Chapter 13. Some embrace Christianity until the precepts of Christ become unpopular with a sinful world, others make Christ a distant second to the pursuit of power and riches, and then there are those who reject popularity and position (Psalm 84:10) and live a life that aligns with the first and greatest commandment (Matt. 22: 36–40).

Not only is Christianity being portrayed in a negative light, but standing on biblical beliefs now brings with it the very persecution and tribulation that Jesus mentioned. Merely stating that one believes marriage is the union of a man and a woman may lead to protests or, for some, the loss of employment.

If current trends continue, I suspect that American Christians will eventually be as hated as Christians in Muslim-majority nations. Although this is a cause for concern, we should not be surprised. Jesus warned that Christians who held to biblical beliefs would be hated for it (John 17:14).

The enemies of Christ are now telling Christians how to practice their faith. We cannot call the murder of the unborn (abortion), "the murder of the unborn", we cannot call immorality and depravity, "immorality and depravity" and if we dare to call a sin "a sin," we are counted as the worst that humanity has to offer. Because Christianity condemns these things in which they participate, they must silence us, redefine them, or both. Again, those who continually call for tolerance of the beliefs and values of others, have no tolerance for Christianity. One example of many is the report of the extremely intelligent sixteen-year-old who was given four zeros by a Polk University professor for not agreeing with his anti-Christian views (Berry, 2015).

Her story is but one of multitudes that the yellow journalists of the mainstream media refuse to report on. Then there is the air force general, a Christian, who had the unmitigated gall to credit God for the successes of his career during a speech at the Christian National Day of Prayer celebrations. Antichrists (atheists), much like the Sadducees and Pharisees of the Bible, were so outraged that he dared to mention God and Jesus called for the General to be court martialed (Bennett, 2015). How dare a practicing Christian, at a Christian service, mention God and Jesus. The ever-so-tolerant left will not tolerate it.

It is stories such as these that should, and probably would, outrage the black church, if only they were reported often enough. But few in the black community would be willing to accept that these instances of Christian persecution are encouraged and supported by the very people that we so loyally support year after year, Democrats. Faced with the truth about our beloved democrats, most will find some way to turn the conversation to blaming former President George Bush, or the racist republicans.

I suspect that most black Christians would reject the fact that it is those whom they mistakenly believe are looking out for us that are in fact, attacking and attempting to outlaw our faith. An article by Coca (2015) illustrates a prime example of how antichrists are attempting to tell Christians how to practice their faith. During a speech meant to justify his passion for stealing from the industrious to give to the lazy, the biggest antichrist in America, BHO, contended that Christians should not oppose the murder of unborn babies (abortion) or the promotion of the state sanctioned-lifestyle of Sodom and Gomorrah (gay marriage). Vice President Biden equates the belief that the lifestyle of Sodom and Gomorrah is a sin with violence (Unruh, 2015) the vice president would have Christians reject biblical precepts and embrace and encourage depravity to our children and our society.

During an April 2015 speech in New York City, Hillary Clinton seemed to suggest that the government should use force to change the views of those who are opposed to the murder of the unborn and the promotion of the lifestyle of Sodom and Gomorrah (Ertelt, 2015). Such a measure, and I suspect that I will see it in my lifetime, would have the effect of criminalizing one's very thoughts. Further confirming her belief that the law should be used as a means to force Christians to change their beliefs, Hillary Clinton, who broke the law by having a private e mail server while serving as secretary of state (Cuccinelli, 2015), contended that jail was the right thing for Kim Davis, who refused to issue same sex marriage licenses (Newsmax, 2015). If Mrs. Davis' crime is not upholding the Constitution of the United States then why aren't BHO, Eric Holder and others behind bars as well? This great concern for enforcing the law is forgotten when BHO and so called "sanctuary cities" choose to ignore the nation's immigration laws. Our immigration laws do not become null and void simply because liberals do not agree with them (*Washington Examiner*, 2015).

BHO seems to contend that if Christians would just embrace these issues and reject scripture, they would draw more followers. But, BHO fails to understand that Christianity is not about numbers or popularity. Scripture clearly states that few will follow the narrow path to salvation. Christianity is about standing for righteousness. Noah, Lot, the Twelve Apostles, Paul, Moses, Daniel and the three Hebrew children all of these great men of the faith were greatly outnumbered by the wicked and chose righteousness over popular culture. Over and over Scripture tells us that the path to salvation is found only by a few. They fail to understand that sin is what God says it is, not what liberals have determined it is not. Like Cain, they want to dictate the way God is to be worshipped; we, like Abel, must worship God according to His will.

AMERICA UNDER THE INFLUENCE

"She has rebelled against My judgments by doing wickedness more than the nations, and against My statutes more than the countries that are all around her; for they have refused My judgments, and they have not walked in My statutes"
(Ezek. 5:6).

Under the influence of those on the left, the nation has experienced a dramatic rise in crime. Murders, violent crimes and sexual assaults have increased in many of the nation's cities. Referred to as "the Ferguson Effect," some believe the crime wave is a result of criminals feeling emboldened by the hostility displayed towards law enforcement officers by BHO, his Department of Justice (DOJ), Al Sharpton, and a biased media (Nolte, 2015). Others suggest the increase in crime is due to "police slowdowns" (Schuppe, 2015). I believe that after seeing what officer Darren Wilson went through for having the audacity to stop, and be forced to kill, a robbery suspect in self-defense, police officers are being much more careful in their approach to crime fighting. The nation has seen that under the Obama administration, enforcing the law when the criminal happens to be a black male may lead to scrutiny, claims of racism, and ultimately charges being filed against police officers. Not only have we witnessed an increase in violent crimes against civilians but murders of police officers increased by an astronomical 89 percent in 2014 (Pavilich, 2015). The murders of police officers began shortly after a march led by professional racist and inciter of deadly riots, Al Sharpton.

Not satisfied that true justice was rendered in the case of officer Darren Wilson, ignoring the fact that he and the Obama administration had inspired the people of Ferguson, Missouri, to loot, burn and destroy their community in defense of a suspect who was clearly shown on video committing the crime for which he was accused, rejecting the eyewitness testimony of those who corroborated officer Wilson's account of his encounter with Michael Brown, the shameless reverend and his followers chanted "What do we want? Dead cops! When do what them? Now!" (Pavilich, 2014). One week later the "reverend riot" and his followers would have their wish as New York Police Department Officers Rafael Ramos and Wenjian Liu would be murdered while sitting in their patrol car.

Since then, a number of police officers nationwide have been assassinated while on duty (Evans and Nakhlawi, 2016). In a sad illustration of race relations under the Obama reign, I've listened as some have tried to justify the assassinations of police officers in Dallas and Baton Rouge. We have certainly seen some instances of police shootings of blacks that I find completely indefensible. The most recent involved the shooting of a therapist, lying on the ground, with his hands in the air, communicating who he was, what he was doing, and that his patient, an autistic young man, did not have a gun (Emery, 2016) yet a responding officer shot him anyway. That officer and that officer alone, should be held accountable for that shooting. Unfortunately, this is not the only incident of an indefensible shooting that has been in the news. But when we begin to blame every man and woman in uniform for the actions of a few, we become guilty of the same sort of profiling that we so often complain about.

To the Democrats and their self-serving servants, so-called black leaders, it's not black lives that matter, it's black deaths. They capitalize on the deaths of blacks, whether it's the high percentage of unborn black babies that they funnel to their murderous allies in the child murdering industry (abortionists), or the criminal law breaker who is killed during the commission of a crime. Each of these deaths presents an opportunity for the self-servers to capitalize on.

They maintain their lofty positions by supporting, rather than opposing, the abortion industries practice of murdering our unborn children. When police officers are called upon to perform their jobs, they capitalize on false claims of racism if the suspect is black, regardless of the facts of the case. And somehow, Republicans are always viewed as the cause of this manufactured racism, motivating blacks to oppose them during election seasons.

Under the influence of those on the left, America seems more like a land colonized by a variety of different nations, rather than a sovereign nation. We've seen several instances of high schools and colleges banning the American flag. On May 5, 2010 (Cinco de Mayo), students at Live Oak High School in Morgan Hill, California, were ordered to remove their clothing that displayed colors of the American flag because it might be offensive to Hispanic students (Chambers, 2015). When family members filed suit, citing a violation of the students' freedom of speech, the Ninth Circuit Court sided with the school. The US Supreme Court, by refusing to hear the appeal, also sided with the school. More recently, members of the University of California-Irvine attempted to ban the American flag from an area of the school claiming that the American flag, on an American campus, in America, is "divisive" and reminds minority students of "colonialism" (Chambers, 2015).

In recent years I have also been reminded of colonialism as America begins to look, and more importantly act, not like a sovereign nation but like a collection of colonies of different nations. And it is rulings and attempts like the previously mentioned two that would ban our flag in favor of those who would reap the benefits and freedoms of America but are more loyal to other nations. Under the influence of those on the left, Americans are now ruled and not represented. Our democracy seems more like a dictatorship, especially under the Obama administration. The citizens of other nations and the Syrian refugees have more representation from our leaders than do the American tax paying citizens.

The wisdom of man, and liberals, says that our differences make us stronger. That sounds very nice; however, the evidence of current society presents a very different reality. We are a nation divide by religion, skin color, sexual preference, citizens and illegal immigrants, and remarkably even, males and females, with some vying for some form of special treatment. Claiming that division (differences) makes us closer, has a nice ring to it but if America is not allowed to be America, I fear that the nation will someday confirm Matthew 12:25, which includes "Every kingdom divided against itself is brought to desolation, and every city or house divided against itself will not stand. Ethnic and racial diversity can be a beautiful thing, but cultural diversity has caused more division. America needs leaders who will stand up and say this is our flag (the American flag), these are our major holidays (Christmas, Easter, Thanksgiving, the 4th of July, et cetera), this is our major religion (Christianity), these are our laws (the laws passed by our lawmakers). You are welcome to live among us, but if you find any of these offensive this might not be the place for you. Why come to America if you want to change it into the land that you voluntarily left?

Unfortunately, we are ruled, not represented, by leaders whose concerns are the wishes of those from other nations, so much so that they are even unwilling to declare that English is America's official language. Our rulers like to justify illegal immigration by claiming that our immigration system is broken It's not, the laws simply need to be enforced. They claim that Washington is broken. It's not; our leaders are simply corrupt, willing to break the laws that they have sworn to uphold, actions that would land the average citizen in jail.

I believe that those in government should be held accountable just like the average citizen, perhaps even face a harsher form of punishment for knowingly breaking the laws that they have sworn to uphold. Too often we have seen government officials commit perjury, take bribes, destroy evidence, even after it has been requested, all with little or no consequences.

After the behavior of some of the nation's attorneys general, specifically Janet Reno, Alberto Gonzalez, Eric Holder and now Loretta Lynch, I believe that our political system would be better served if the opposition party appointed the nation's attorney general. Under our current system, attorneys general have shown that they are willing to overlook the deeds of those who appointed them and cannot be fair and objective. Saying no one is above the law has a righteous ring to it; however, much too often, it seems as if those who craft the laws, especially if their named Clinton, are free to ignore them.

PERSONAL RESPONSIBILITY

*"And Elijah came to all the people, and said, 'How long will
you falter between two opinions? If the Lord is God, follow
Him; but if Baal, follow him.' But the people answered
him not a word"
(1 Kings 18:21).*

I've been very critical of what passes for black leadership and critical of the churches that have given more honor to a political party than to the God that they gather to serve every Sunday. But, what of we the people? Do we bear any responsibility when it comes to the self- destructive policies that we continue to support? Of course we do. Someone once said that people deserve the government that they get. I'm not sure that that's the case when it comes to brutal dictatorships but, I do believe it applies to truly democratic nations.

Even in America, with our pseudo democracy of delegates and super delegates, where both major parties attempt to water down the will of the people with their rigged systems, the will of the people should be the deciding factor when it comes to choosing leaders. During this election cycle (2016) we've seen both major parties attempt to undermine the will of the people. The Democrats were successful in their attempts to undermine the campaign of Bernie Sanders; however, the Republicans failed in their attempts to derail the campaign of Donald Trump.

When the subject of politics comes up and I've made my views known, much to the astonishment of some, I'm usually asked how it can be that I, a black man, refuses to support the Democrat Party. My answer is that they are constantly trying to pass legislation that would outlaw my faith, a faith in the one true God, all while praising and uplifting the other false gods of polytheistic America. My allegiance to Jesus Christ is stronger than any ties to a political affiliation; The Democrat Party members are constantly encouraging the promotion of the lifestyle of Sodom and Gomorrah among the nation and our young and they support, defend, and encourage the murders of unborn and newly born babies.

Not only do we, blacks support the self-destructive policies of the Democrats, but we expect every other black person to blindly support them also. When Al Gore was running against George Bush, a union official at my former place of employment was so astonished that I would not be supporting the advocate for child murder, Al Gore, that he questioned my blackness. "Wait a minute," he exclaimed, "who's supposed to be the black man here, me or you?" I promptly explained to this union official, a white man, that I was not born into a political party. And that for me the admonition of Scripture to love the Lord thy God with all my heart soul and mind, that "mankind shall not lie with mankind as with womankind, and thou shalt commit no murders, supersedes political affiliation, skin color, nationality, and even familial ties.

Recently, a female friend of mine was telling me that she couldn't stand Alan Keyes or Clarence Thomas. When I asked why she said of Keyes "Because he says negative things about Obama." When I asked if she had ever investigated or even considered that Mr. Keyes's statements were true, she didn't answer, preferring to restate that she doesn't like Mr. Keyes. My dear friend thus answered the question posed in Galatians 4:16. *"Have I therefore become your enemy because I tell you the truth?"* (Gal. 4:16). And she confirmed Amos 5:10, *"They hate the one who rebukes in the gate, and they abhor the one who speaks uprightly"* (Amos 5:10). When she discovered that I was not a supporter of the newly elected Barack Hussein Obama, she was also

THOUGH THEY SLAY US, STILL WILL WE TRUST THEM

baffled, "I don't understand how you, being black, cannot support Obama." she said, similar to the words recently spoken during the debate concerning healthcare reform by the attention-loving Jesse Jackson, who declared that a person cannot be black and oppose this legislation (Soraghan, 2009).

When it comes to the illogical relationship between blacks and liberal democrats, I used to find some consolation in the verse of scripture that says my people are destroyed for lack of knowledge. *"My people are destroyed for lack of knowledge. Because you have rejected knowledge, I also will reject you from being priest for Me; Because you have forgotten the law of your God, I also will forget your children"* *(Hosea 4:6).* I used to think that if only blacks were aware of the types of policies that we support by allying ourselves with the Democrat party that we would quickly withdraw our support. But, sadly, as I have tried to inform anyone who is willing to listen about the fruits of our support for the Democrat party I've come to the realization that many, indeed, most, have chosen instead to reject knowledge; that every two years most will forget about the laws of the God that we say we serve, and strengthen the hands of those who are in direct opposition to that God.

The sad truth is that most in the black community have preferred to believe lies put forth by the Democrat leadership and their overseers in the black leadership. When George Bush was running for his second term, I had a conversation with a young lady, about the upcoming election. She was eagerly anticipating President Bush's defeat and was surprised that I was supporting him. After I had explained my reasons for supporting President Bush and my reasons for opposing the Democratic candidate, the rejection of Christ, the promotion of perversion, the murder of unborn and newly born babies, and the destruction of the black family and the potential of our young, I asked the young lady if her views had now changed. The only answer I got was a telling smile. That smile told me that no matter what the Democrats did, this young lady, like 90 to 95 percent of the black community would support them, regardless.

When another friend wanted to know how it was possible that I didn't support the Democrats, I explained that I could not support antichrists, sexual deviants, and child murderers. When I asked her what was her reason for supporting them she replied that they had always been there for blacks and done a lot for blacks. When I asked her to list some of the things that they've done to benefit blacks, she had no answers.

When Bill Clinton was accused of having sexual relations with Monica Lewinsky, I listened as those around me vehemently defended this first black president. "The Republicans are making up lies about Clinton because he's done so much for the black community" was the typical statement. But, I agree with the assessment BHO's former pastor, Jeremiah Wright, of how much Bill Clinton helped the black community. In effect, Bill Clinton has done the same thing to the black community that he did to Monica Lewinsky. To us adults the Reverend Wright's meaning was quite clear. For far too many of us, Bill Clinton's supposedly knowing the words to the national black anthem, being able to play the saxophone, playing golf with Vernon Jordan, and using Betty Currie to shuttle Monica Lewinsky to and from the Oval Office count somehow as a great boon for the black community.

While taking a history class in which we covered the period during which slavery occurred some of my fellow students expressed their anger about the way in which blacks were treated during that period. In a discussion with one young lady she said she even dropped the class because the topic of slavery made her so angry. I expressed to one of the young ladies that I could well understand her anger and asked her if the brutality faced by our people so many years ago made her so angry shouldn't we be at least as angry about what the Democrat Party are doing to the blacks here in the present? Outlawing our faith, murdering our unborn, corrupting the morals of our young and condemning our children to a substandard education? She, as expected, failed to see the similarity.

Another Bible verse that sheds some light onto why blacks are so zealous about supporting a group that promote the very things we claim to be against, the destruction of the God ordained institution of marriage, and the murder of millions of unborn babies, is Proverbs 22:6. *"Train up a child in the way he should go: and when he is old he will not depart from it* (Prov. 22:6).

We usually look at this verse from a positive standpoint but it can be applied either for good or for evil. Just like BHO's election mantra of "change" we've learned that not all change is good. Neither is all training. If a child is trained up to follow evil habits, when he is old he will also not depart from the evil. From an early age blacks are taught to believe that all Republicans are racists. This teaching comes from the Democrat party, through their designated overseers in the so called "black leadership" and as Obama's former church illustrated to the nation, even though some churches.

We have been trained by the democrats about what to think and even what to say. As I listen to those defending the policies of the white house they spew forth the same rhetoric as Obama and the democrats. "He needs more time" they say, "He inherited this mess from the Bush administration," they contend. "People oppose his policies because he's black," they claim.

As BHO himself admitted, in a rare moment of honesty, he was black when some of these same people voted for him. We have become so well versed in parroting what the democrats say and blaming George Bush for everything wrong under the sun that one young black lady, during a televised Frank Luntz focus group on the Fox News Channel, discussing the BP oil spill, had no qualms about placing the blame for the Gulf oil disaster squarely on the shoulders of former President Bush.

We prefer to believe lies about who were the true slave holders, who fought for and who opposed civil rights for blacks. And with those on the left hand shamefully re writing history, and the Republicans unwilling to refute their lies, it's no wonder that blacks believe these lies about the past. I was well into my thirties before I discovered that the Republican party was founded specifically to oppose slavery.

And this is no endorsement of a Republican leadership that has increasingly begun to resemble the liberal Democrats. A Republican leadership whose treatment of Christians is much like the Democrats' treatment of blacks. They pretend to be concerned about the issues that are important to us, then after we help to get them elected, they abandon us and our concerns. A Republican leadership that instead of arguing for the enforcement of our current immigration laws, agree that those who have broken them should be rewarded, that join those on the left hand in defining the murder of unborn children as *choice, women's health, reproductive freedom*, and a *right to privacy* and that equate a chosen behavior, homosexuality, with being born black or minority.

A Republican leadership that lets liberals or their surrogates decide on the conditions, locations, and persons moderating presidential debates. Even birds know to avoid a trap when it's laid out in plain sight (Proverbs 1:17). Not so this republican leadership. Arlen Spector may be dead and gone but his spirit still lives on in members of the Republican Party.

Our loyalty, ladies and gentlemen who profess Jesus Christ, should be to Jesus Christ and his father who sent him. Remember the first and great commandment, *"Jesus said to him, 'You shall love the Lord your God with all your heart, with all your soul, and with all your mind.' This is the first and great commandment. And the second is like it: 'You shall love your neighbor as yourself* (Matt. 22:37–39). And what of the helpless unborn? Are they not our neighbors?

Sadly, as I've found myself forced to defend my opposition to those whose policies and appointees have the intent of outlawing Christ, encouraging the murder of innocent babies, and spreading the lifestyle of Sodom and Gomorrah, I've found myself in heated debates with fellow Christians. The sad part is that a few, counted among the best people that I know, during these heated debates have admitted that regardless of scripture, they will continue to cast their support behind the Democrat Party, those who's every policy seems to be aimed at the destruction of the Christian faith, innocent life, and any semblance of morality that our constantly morally decaying nation tries to cling to.

A few weeks after the killing of Osama Bin Laden, a friend of mine expressed how annoyed he was with the media because they seemed to be giving seal team six more credit for eliminating Bin Laden than Obama. While I agreed that Obama deserved a great deal of credit for eliminating Bin Laden, some of his predecessors or those in their administration had previously passed up opportunities to either take custody of or eliminate terrorists in the past because they didn't want to hurt the enemy's feelings, and I applaud his actions. But, to declare the actions of someone who sat in an office and watched the operation on video with the actions of those brave individuals who invaded the stronghold of a murderous terrorist mastermind, in a nation suspected of aiding terrorists is , in my estimation, ridiculous.

My friend soon discovered that I was no fan of Obama or his party. As I laid out my reasons for opposing the party who is hostile to Christ, promoters of child murderers and promoters of the lifestyle of Sodom and Gomorrah, I backed them up with scripture. After a heated debate my good friend conceded that scripture was right but, that he has supported Obama and the democrats and he would continue to do so. He, like far too many, has chosen to lay aside the doctrine of Christ for the tradition men. And by his words this young man, who attends church religiously, confirmed the verse of scripture that states you cannot serve two masters *"No one can serve two masters; for either he will hate the one and love the other, or else he will be loyal to the one and despise the other. You cannot serve God and mammon* (Matt. 6:24). But, it is not money that he has elevated above God, it is political affiliation.

During a heated debate with another gentleman, again considered one of the best people I know, this gentleman admitted his strong opposition to equating the lifestyle of Sodom and Gomorrah with biblical marriage, and an opposition to murdering unborn children. When I explained to him that these were exactly the things that he was supporting through his support of liberal democrats he became very hostile and stated that regardless of these positions supported by the Democrats, he would *Never, Ever* vote for anyone who is a Republican.

In yet another discussion with a very religious lady, who reminds me of the virtuous woman from scripture, except for her die-hard support for the powers and principalities of the Democrat party, as she was criticizing those who opposed Obama's policies, I explained my reasons, backed by scripture, for opposing BHO's policies and wondered how anyone who claimed to follow the Christ that Obama was so hostile to could support Obama. But, she also, like my good friend and the previously mentioned gentleman became angry and stated that she would always support the Democrat Party and could never vote for any Republican.

Completely lost on my good friend, the previously mentioned gentleman, and this religious woman is the effect of their statements. When they acknowledge that counting Christ among the transgressors, murdering unborn and newly born children and promoting the lifestyle of Sodom and Gomorrah are wicked deeds but, declare that they will always support those who are promoting and defending these acts, they are effectively saying, "Nevertheless Democrat Party, your will be done and not that of the God of creation.

They are effectively saying we will obey man and not God. They are rendering to a political party the things that should be rendered unto God. They have embraced Obama's attempts at change, changing the country's foundation, changing the nation's motto and changing the God ordained institution of marriage, and rejected the righteousness of God. *My son, fear the Lord and the king; Do not associate with those given to change* (Prov. 24:21).

Finally, these precious, precious people have taken the counsel of a political party and rejected the instructions of the God of creation. *"Woe to the rebellious children," says the Lord, "Who take counsel, but not of Me, and who devise plans, but not of My Spirit, that they may add sin to sin* (Isaiah 30:1).

When it comes to the dictates of those on the left hand, the black community's position can be summed up by loosely paraphrasing a quote of Alfred, Lord Tennyson, "Ours is not to reason why, ours is not to make reply, ours is but to do and to die." We do not question why they have condemned our children to underperforming schools, when they force the lifestyle of Sodom and Gomorrah down our throats or reply is that we don't agree with them but we will support them, and when they demand the lives of our unborn children we willingly sacrifice them.

Many of us often look back at the past and proclaim what we would have done had we lived during certain time periods. We would have stood by Jesus, we would have fought for the freedom of the slaves, we would have helped the Jews. And yet, here in our own period of history we have an opportunity to oppose the daily slaughter of thousands of unborn babies and instead we strengthen the hands of their executioners.

Will we be like the scribes and Pharisees who proclaimed what good deeds they would have done had they lived in the time of their fathers all while they continued to persecute the righteous men sent to them by God. During the past two presidential elections we had the rare opportunity to support candidates who held biblical world views. Candidates who did not apologize for nor were ashamed of their faiths in Christ.

In 2008 Mike Huckabee, and during the 2012 presidential campaign both Michelle Bachman and Rick Santorum, presented us with candidates who held godly positions. But rather than support them we attacked them, ridiculed them, and accused them of being racists. When the honorable Ambassador Alan Keyes, a black man who held strong Christian values, ran for president we also rejected him, proving that the Democrat Party takes precedence over skin color as well as Christ.

But such is the plight of those who boldly cling to Christian values, even their own party, the Republicans will seek to distance themselves from any who hold Christian values. This election season once again, presented us with candidates who were not ashamed of their faith in Christ, former Governor Mike Huckabee, Dr. Ben Carson, and former senator Rick Santorum, but because they are associated with the republican party, they were not even considered by black Christians. Because they are not Democrats, most black Christians would oppose them in favor of a proven liar, a power hungry individual who for years subjected women to psychological torture as she protected and enabled a sexual predator, Hillary Clinton.

NOTHING NEW UNDER THE SUN

Once again, in the book of Ecclesiastes Solomon tells us that there is nothing new under the sun.

Is there anything of which it may be said, "See, this is new"? It has already been in ancient times before (Eccl. 1:10).

Amazingly we can recognize the actions of the wicked in the bible but, in our own lives we zealously support and defend those very same acts. Those on the left hand have re packaged those acts that scripture so strongly condemns and called them laws and constitutional rights. Following the example of the religious leaders of Christ's time, re packaged as a separation of church and state, they prohibit even the mention of Jesus' name. *So they called them and commanded them not to speak at all nor teach in the name of Jesus* (Acts 4:18).

Taking a page from Pharaoh's book they have appointed themselves controllers of the population. And the main targets of their population control have been their most loyal supporters, the black community. *So Pharaoh commanded all his people, saying, "Every son who is born you shall cast into the river, and every daughter you shall save alive"* (Exod. 1:22). While Pharaoh spared the female babies, the Democrats and Planned Parenthood show mercy to none, male nor female.

But, where Pharaoh feared that the Jews would one day join his enemies, liberal Democrats are motivated by the belief that blacks are a tremendous deficit to society. That we are a waste of society's resources, that we are destined for lives of crime and poverty. They believe, like one of their most revered heroes, Planned Parenthood founder Margaret Sanger, that the world would be a better place if we were simply not born. To that end they have, amazingly, enlisted the aid of black leaders and black churches to aid in realizing Margaret Sanger's demonic vision for blacks by ensuring the continuation of the murder of our unborn. These murderous acts they have renamed *women's health issues, a right to privacy, reproductive freedom,* and *choice.* They have taken the legitimate medical term *abortion* and used it to sugarcoat the murder of unborn children. And in a brutal and heartless imitation of Pharaoh and of the great red dragon of Revelation 12:4, they have ended the lives of newly born babies and repackaged the murderous acts as partial-birth abortion.

The lifestyle of Sodom and Gomorrah that scripture calls ungodly, depraved and lawless they have repackaged as a safe, natural, healthy alternative lifestyle.

> *And turning the cities of Sodom and Gomorrah into ashes, condemned them to destruction, making them an example to those who afterward would live ungodly; and delivered righteous Lot, who was oppressed by the filthy conduct of the wicked (for that righteous man, dwelling among them, tormented his righteous soul from day to day by seeing and hearing their lawless deeds* (2 Peter 2:6–8).

Like the mythical vampire, they recoil at the sight of the cross. It is often preached that demons tremble at the mention of Jesus name, well so to do these democrats. At the very mention of Jesus' name, they and their supporters cry foul. And more often than not, their attack dogs in the ACLU (whom I call "Anti-Christian Lawyers United") file lawsuits to silence and punish any who dare to even mention the name of Jesus. These are the things championed by the Dems. It is inconsistent to claim Christ and support these acts. To do so would make political affiliation one's god.

Furthermore, black community, you who profess Christ must heed the words of the apostle John, *"If anyone comes to you and does not bring this doctrine, do not receive him into your house nor greet him; or he who greets him shares in his evil deeds* (2 John 1:10, 11).

According to this verse, all those who knowingly support evil individuals and their deeds, are viewed in the eyes of God as accessories to their sins. Accessories to attacks on the cross of Christ, to hostility towards God's chosen people, Israel, accessories to the murders of millions and millions of innocent babes. We have made ourselves accessories to the murders of every unborn and newly born baby that this party has enabled and encouraged and we have become accessories to the promotion of the lifestyle of Sodom and Gomorrah.

And if he that supports a prophet will receive a prophet's reward, what can we expect for those that support the enemies of Christ, the shedding of innocent blood and the promotion of the lifestyle of Sodom and Gomorrah. We can expect that those who support such people will receive the same reward as they. We should serve God and not political affiliation. And please, let us not deceive ourselves currently we are serving political affiliation.

Was Job's dedication to God any stronger than ours is to the Democrats? If the black community were as zealous in their defense of Christ as we are in our defense and support of the Democrat party, our station in society would be much better. Our children would be better educated, our numbers would be much greater and the stability that the black family once enjoyed, during much more difficult times, would be returned. But, we have trusted a political party and rejected God. And while God wants what's best for us; the Democrats view us only as merchandise. Under the influence of those on the left hand America has become like the houses of Israel and Judah, we are full of blood and perversion.

> *"Then He said to me, "The iniquity of the house of Israel and Judah is exceedingly great, and the land is full of bloodshed, and the city full of perversity; for they say, 'The Lord has forsaken the land, and the Lord does not see"* (Ezek. 9:9)! And our support

of those on the left hand has been instrumental in bringing America to this point.

We continue to listen to their words while turning a blind eye to their deeds. A famous quote by Englishman Sir Edmund Burke states "The only thing necessary for the triumph of evil is for good men to do nothing." How much more will evil spread when good men actually support it? Scripture commands that we hate the evil and love the good. *"Hate evil, love good; establish justice in the gate. It may be that the Lord God of hosts Will be gracious to the remnant of Joseph" (Amos 5: 15).* But we have done the opposite.

I write these things not as some paragon of virtue. We know from Scripture that if any man claims that he is not a sinner he is a liar. *If we say that we have no sin, we deceive ourselves, and the truth is not in us. If we confess our sins, He is faithful and just to forgive us our sins and to cleanse us from all unrighteousness. If we say that we have not sinned, we make Him a liar, and His word is not in us* (1 John 1:8–10).

But I write these things out of a love for a people who have chosen friendship with the world over the word of God. A people who will acknowledge that God is righteous but still support policies clearly contrary to his word. *For out of much affliction and anguish of heart I wrote to you, with many tears, not that you should be grieved, but that you might know the love which I have so abundantly for you* (2 Cor. 2:4).

It is extremely frustrating to stand by and watch as so many good (by man's standards) people choose to stand with those on the left hand. And if we stand with them now, in opposition to the commandments of the creator, we will certainly stand with them at the judgement.

Then He will also say to those on the left hand, 'Depart from Me, you cursed, into the everlasting fire prepared for the devil and his angels: for I was hungry and you gave Me no food; I was thirsty and you gave Me no drink; I was a stranger and you did not take Me in, naked and you did not clothe Me, sick and in prison and you did not visit Me.' "Then they also will answer Him, saying, 'Lord, when did we see You hungry or thirsty or a stranger or naked or sick or in prison, and did not minister to You?' Then He will answer them, saying, 'Assuredly, I say to you, inasmuch as you did not do it to one of the least of these, you did not do it to Me.' And these will go away into everlasting punishment, but the righteous into eternal life" (Matt. 25:41–46).

This blind devotion to a political party has become our Babylon and the God of creation is calling us out from among them.

Do not be unequally yoked together with unbelievers. For what fellowship has righteousness with lawlessness? And what communion has light with darkness? And what accord has Christ with Belial? Or what part has a believer with an unbeliever? And what agreement has the temple of God with idols? For you are the temple of the living God. As God has said: "I will dwell in them and walk among them. I will be their God, and they shall be My people." Therefore "Come out from among them and be separate, says the Lord. Do not touch what is unclean, and I will receive you. I will be a Father to you, and you shall be My sons and daughters, Says the Lord Almighty" (2 Cor. 6:14–18).

We have been, and are, as devoted to this political party as Job was to God, though they slay us, still after many decades, we continue to trust them. *"Though He slay me, yet will I trust Him. Even so, I will defend my own ways before Him"* (Job 13:15).

It is no great coincidence that those who exhibit hostility to Christ, promote the murder of unborn babies, and promote the lifestyle of Sodom and Gomorrah are called those on the left. Scripture also identifies the unrighteous as "those on the left hand." *"Then He will also say to those on the left hand, 'Depart from Me, you cursed, into the everlasting fire prepared for the devil and his angels* (Matt. 25:41).

As I've debated friends and family about who we choose to support and why, I'm often told that the good thing about America is that everyone is entitled to their own opinion. But, scripture was given to instruct us to keep us on the paths of righteousness. *"All scripture is given by inspiration of God, and is profitable for doctrine, for reproof, for correction, for instruction in righteousness"* (2 Tim. 3:16*).* In the eyes of God, we are either with Him, contending for the faith, promoting life, and promoting morality or we are against him, counting Christ among the transgressors (separation of Christ and state), promoting the murders of unborn and newly born babies (abortion) and promoting the lifestyle of Sodom and Gomorrah (homosexuality) *"He who is not with Me is against Me, and he who does not gather with Me scatters abroad"* (Matt. 12:30).

> *"Whoever transgresses and does not abide in the doctrine of Christ does not have God. He who abides in the doctrine of Christ has both the Father and the Son"* (2 John 1:9).

Finally, we, black evangelicals, are not like the politicians that we support. We do not believe in the things they believe in, outlawing Jesus Christ, murdering the unborn, forcing the lifestyle practiced by the citizens of Sodom and Gomorrah on the entire nation, and institutionalizing lower academic standards for black students. Yet, through tradition and emotional manipulation we still support them, never questioning their policies or the results of over 50 years of those policies.

We are the confirmation of Proverbs 22:6. *Train up a child in the way he should go: and when he is old he will not depart from it.* If we love God, and I believe we do, shouldn't his commandments supersede those of liberal democrats? *"If you love me keep my commandments"* (John 14:15). God has not presented us with riddles and difficult choices when it comes to how we should live and who we should support. If life were a test of multiple choices, God has given us the answers. When it comes to good and evil, he instructs us to *Hate evil, love good; establish justice in the gate. It may be that the Lord God of hosts will be gracious to the remnant of Joseph* (Amos 5:15).

When it comes to issues of life and death we read *I call heaven and earth as witnesses today against you, that I have set before you life and death, blessing and cursing; therefore choose life, that both you and your descendants may live* (Deut. 30:19). And yet, Democrats ensure that hundreds of millions of dollars are awarded to a group of butchers who use it to murder, in the most barbaric and torturous ways, unborn and newly born children. They have even resorted to selling the body parts of these babies. *Also their bows will dash the young men to pieces, and they will have no pity on the fruit of the womb; Their eye will not spare children* (Isa. 13:18).

When it comes to choosing the nation's leaders we are instructed *Moreover you shall select from all the people able men, such as fear God, men of truth, hating covetousness; and place such over them to be rulers of thousands, rulers of hundreds, rulers of fifties, and rulers of tens* (Ex. 18:21). We cannot serve God while supporting antichrists, child murderers, and the immoral. And finally, he has even identified the wicked as those on the left. The same term used to describe liberal and progressive democrats. "*Then He will also say to those on the left hand, 'Depart from Me, you cursed, into the everlasting fire prepared for the devil and his angels*" (Matthew 25:41).

At the judgment, God will make no distinction between us and those that we've empowered. *Whoever transgresses and does not abide in the doctrine of Christ does not have God. He who abides in the doctrine of Christ has both the Father and the Son. If anyone comes to you and does not bring this doctrine, do not receive him into your house nor greet him; for he who greets him shares in his evil deeds* (2 John 1:9–11).

Just like the rebellious Israelites made a molten calf and presented it to the people as their God (Exod. 23:7–8) so-called black leaders, a liberal media, and, sadly, even some pastors have presented the Democrat's jackass as the god of the African-American community. Aided with our blind support, the enemies of Christ have molded America into a nation where truth is considered offensive, morality considered hateful, and Jesus Christ considered a menace. The God-ordained institution of marriage is called hateful and discriminatory, the body parts of murdered babies are bought and sold like merchandise, the wicked feel justified in demanding that grown men and boys have access to the same restrooms, dorm rooms, and showers as our wives and young daughters, and the mere mention of Jesus' name is considered a crime.

All these things the wicked have achieved while boasting that we, the black community, are their most loyal supporters. However, we are not like those that we support, we do not agree with the results of their policies and yet, we support them still. We have given them the type of trust that Job reserved for God alone, and for decades they have abused that trust. We have allowed them to do our thinking for us. They have successfully convinced us to turn on any who would dare to point out their bitter betrayal. Those who choose Christ over party will suffer persecution (2 Tim. 3:12).

> *When the world seems against you and troubles are many, you look for support but fail to find any. Remember the words the savior left with us, mankind will hate you, if in Christ you trust. So look to the skies, and rest most assured, in the eyes of the Father you are adored. You may lose some battles, all hope seem undone, but if in Christ you trust, you've already won.*

America's hope lies in God, not government. America can achieve the ideals set out in our founding documents, documents that admit a reliance on the creator of the universe. But, it will require that Christians stand up and contend for the faith (Jude 3). It will require that Christians of all creeds and colors come out of the shadows, come out of the closets, and declare to the nation and the world that we will not apologize for our faith, nor are we ashamed of our faith in Christ.

Each passing day brings us closer to Christ's return, if we stand with those on the left hand now, we will have earned our place by their side at the day of judgment. *"Then He will also say to those on the left hand, 'Depart from Me, you cursed, into the everlasting fire prepared for the devil and his angels"* (Matt.25:41).

ENDNOTES

CHAPTER 1

1   Kirsanow, 2011
2   Washington, 2012
3   Gardner, 2008
4   Bumiller, 2008
5   Peterson, 2008
6   Osteens: Obama Doing Great Job, Loves the Lord, 2009
7   Sahgal, N., & Smith, G. 2009
8   *"Surely in vain the net is spread in the sight of any bird"* Proverbs 1:17.
9   Johnson et al., 2004
10 Watkins, 2011
11 NBRA, 2009
12 Malloy, 2014
13 Schraffenberger, 2013
14 The Black Codes, n.d.
15 Radical Reconstruction, n.d.
16 Pickens, 2013
17 Compromise of 1877, 2004
18 The Black Codes, n.d.
19 Williamson, 2012
20 Senate Historical Office, n.d.
21 Freerepublic.com, 2012
22 Blackpast.org, 2011
23 Striewalt, 2015

24 Washingtontimes.com, 2004

25 Korb, 2013

26 Soraghan, 2009

27 Farah, 2004

28 Fund, 2009

29 "Investigation of 'antiwhite bias' grows," Worldnet Daily. com, posted: 7/6/2010,

30 Blankenship, 2009

31 EduWonk, 2005. See also "How the Democrats Destroyed Detroit," *FrontpageMag*, 3/4/2013.

32 Lillis, 2011

33 Freiburger, 2013

34 "The Origins of the Republican Party", 2013

35 Eberle, 2015

36 Beamon, 2015

CHAPTER 2

1 Massie, 2015

2 Downs, 2013

3 Yonke, 2015

4 Elasah Drogin, *Margaret Sanger, Father of Modern Society*, 3rd edition, CUL Publications, 1989, p. 25

5 www.dianedew.com/sanger.htm

6 Kirsanow, 2012.

7 Ertfelt, 2011.

8 Peter J. Smith, "107-count criminal case begins against Planned Parenthood in Kansas," Lifesitenews.com; posted: 2/16/11.

9 Ertfelt, 2011

10 Ostrowski, 2015

11 Unruh, 2015

12 Unruh, 2015

13 Ertelt, 2015

14 Gallagher, 2015
15 Ertelt, 2015
16 Schuberg, 2009
17 Marr, 2005
18 Zahn, 2009

CHAPTER 3

1   "W.E.B. Du Bois, "The Talented Tenth", n.d.
2   Clegg, 2012
3   Bovard, 2014
4   Chumley, 2014
5   Obama Attempts to Suppress Ohio Military Vote, 2012
6   Flynn, 2012
7   Timm, 2013
8   Parker, 2006
9   Martin, 2009
10 Ertelt, 2013
11 Hudson, 2011
12 Cohn, 2003
13 Powe, 2013
14 Soraghan, 2009
15 Miller and Torriero, 2001
16 Jesse Jackson Exposed, 2006
17 Update, 2010
18 Graves, 2012
19 Elder, 2012
20 Jarvie, 2006
21 Rosenbaum and Abraham, 2011
22 Balan, 2010
23 Vega, 2014

CHAPTER 4

1   Allen, 2014
2   Moyer, 2015

3   Sanchez, 2015
4   Hanchett, 2015
5   Farah, 2005
6   Becker & Mcintire, 2015
7   Bennet, 1998
8   Maroney, 2012
9   Sakuma 2015
10 Pepper 2010
11 Obama defends plan to build mosque near ground zero. 2010, August 14. Retrieved November 17, 2014, from http://www.nbcnews.com/id/38698500/ns/politics-white_house/t/obama-defends-plan-build-mosque-near-ground-zero/#.VGmhpyx0zmQ
12 Corsi 2010
13 Debt ceiling skyrockets, Obama no longer calls Bush 'unpatriotic' for increases. 2012, January 30. Retrieved November 18, 2014, from http://www.foxnews.com/politics/2012/01/30/as-debt-ceiling-skyrockets-obama-no-longer-calling-bush-increases-unpatriotic/
14 Fox News, 2015
15 Hohmann 2015
16 Swoyer 2015
17 Hickford 2015
18 Bennett 2015
19 Grider 2013
20 WND 2009
21 Newman, 2015
22 Ibid.
23 Colvin 2015
24 Shapiro 2015
25 Straub, n.d.
26 Is Declaration of Independence unconstitutional? 2004, November 23. Retrieved November 18, 2014, from http://www.wnd.com/2004/11/27718/

27 Black Panther Boss Who Got Off For Voter Intimidation Arrested - Judicial Watch. 2013, June 28. Retrieved November 18, 2014, from http://www.judicialwatch.org/blog/2013/06/black-panther-boss-who-got-off-for-voter-intimidation-arrested/

28 Valdes 2011

29 Cunningham 2012

30 Kline 2011

31 Vadum 2012

32 US shares blame for Mexico drug violence, Clinton says. 2009, March 26. Retrieved November 18, 2014, from http://www.cnn.com/2009/POLITICS/03/25/clinton.mexico/index.html?eref=ib_us

33 Operation Fast and Furious Fast Facts 2014

34 Klein 2012

35 Bump 2016

REFERENCES

Black Men No Better off Than They Were 40 Years Ago. 2014, August 14. Retrieved November 17, 2014, from https://www.popularresistance.org/black-men-no-better-off-than-they-were-40-years-ago/

1871 Congressman Joseph H. Rainey, "Speech Made in Reply to an Attack Upon the Colored State Legislators of South Carolina..." | The Black Past: Remembered and Reclaimed. n.d. Retrieved November 27, 2014, from http://www.blackpast.org/1871-joseph-h-rainey-speech-made-reply-attack-upon-colored-state-legislators-south-carolina

Senate Historical Office. n.d. Retrieved November 27, 2014, from https://www.senate.gov/artandhistory/history/minute/Civil_Rights_Filibuster_Ended.htm

New Wright Ad Attacks Obama in Battlegrounds. 2008, October 27. Retrieved November 20, 2014, from http://abcnews.go.com/blogs/politics/2008/10/new-wright-ad-a/

White House, NASA, Defend Comments About NASA Outreach to Muslim World Criticized by Conservatives. 2010, July 6. Retrieved November 17, 2014, from http://abcnews.go.com/blogs/politics/2010/07/white-house-nasa-defend-comments-about-nasa-outreach-to-muslim-world-criticized-by-conservatives/

President Obama Asks Medvedev for 'Space' on Missile Defense—'After My Election I Have More Flexibility'. 2012, March 26. Retrieved November 19, 2014, from http://abcnews.go.com/blogs/politics/2012/03/president-obama-asks-medvedev-for-space-on-missile-defense-after-my-election-i-have-more-flexibility/

Mozilla CEO Brendan Eich Resigns After Protests from Gay Marriage Supporters. 2014, April 3. Retrieved November 21, 2014, from http://abcnews.go.com/Business/mozilla-ceo-resigns-calif-gay-marriage-ban-campaign/story?id=23181711

Solidarity in Charleston before Church Victims' Funerals - AOL.com. 2015, June 22. Retrieved July 30, 2015, from http://www.aol.com/article/2015/06/22/solidarity-in-charleston-before-church-victims-funerals/21199357/

Clinton says Jail Was 'Right Thing' for Kentucky Clerk. 2015. Retrieved November 11, 2015, from http://www.aol.com/article/2015/10/07/clinton-says-jail-was-right-thing-for-kentucky-clerk/21246278/?icid=maing-grid7|main5|dl5|sec1_lnk2&pLid=292804073

Trump Condemned for Not Correcting Statement Obama is Muslim. 2015. Retrieved December 30, 2015, from http://www.aol.com/article/2015/09/18/trump-condemned-for-not-correcting-statement-obama-is-muslim/21238074/

FBI Says No Way to Check Refugees Coming to US; While Obama Issues This Statement - Allen B. West - AllenBWest.com. 2015, November 15. Retrieved December 30, 2015, from http://www.allenbwest.com/2015/11/fbi-says-no-way-to-check-refugees-coming-to-us-while-obama-issues-this-statement/

Complete Madness: As Paris Mourns, Obama Just Did the UNTHINKABLE - Allen B. West - AllenBWest.com. 2015,

November 16. Retrieved December 30, 2015, from http://www.allenbwest.com/2015/11/complete-madness-as-paris-mourns-obama-just-did-the-unthinkable/

Articles: Obama versus Jesus: Black Christians Must Decide. 2012, August 28. Retrieved November 25, 2014, from http://www.americanthinker.com/articles/2012/08/obama_versus_jesus_black_christians_must_decide.html

Mfume Endorses PETA Campaign. 2003, September 12. Retrieved November 15, 2014, from http://articles.baltimoresun.com/2003-09-12/business/0309120172_1_mfume-peta-kentucky-fried-chicken

Black Mother Jailed for Sending Kids to White School District. 2011, January 25. Retrieved November 25, 2014, from http://www.blackeconomicdevelopment.com/black-mother-jailed-for-sending-kids-to-white-school-district/

70 Pastors Got It Wrong... 1 Got It Right. 2010. Retrieved November 25, 2014, from http://blackquillandink.com/?p=10418

Bovard, J. Education Goals Are Getting Resegregated: Column. 2014. Retrieved February 08, 2016, from http://www.usatoday.com/story/opinion/2014/05/08/education-minorities-blacks-schools-achievement-gap-standards-column/8866485/

FAA Ban Lifted But. 2014, July 24. Retrieved November 23, 2014, from http://www.breakingisraelnews.com/18893/faa-ban-lifted-damage-may-already-done/#uOoq7QrSf7RFj1KR.97

'Ferguson Effect': America's New Crime Wave Is All Part of the Plan - Breitbart. 2015, May 30. Retrieved June 4, 2015, from http://www.breitbart.com/big-government/2015/05/30/ferguson-effect-americas-new-crime-wave-is-all-part-of-the-plan/

CNN's Banfield: Hillary's Emails 'Not Even a Scandal,' That's 'The Republicans' Word For It' - Breitbart. 2015, October 9.

Retrieved November 12, 2015, from http://www.breitbart. com/video/2015/10/09/cnns-banfield-hillarys-emails-not-even-a-scandal-thats-the-republicans-word-for-it/

Geller: Obama's Jihad Against Americans - Breitbart. 2015, November 19. Retrieved December 30, 2015, from http:// www.breitbart.com/big-government/2015/11/19/geller-obamas-jihad-against-americans/

House Chairman: ISIS Tried to Get Into US Via Refugee Program. 2015, December 7. Retrieved December 30, 2015, from http:// www.breitbart.com/big-government/2015/12/07/house-security-chairman-isis-tried-use-refugee-program-get-u-s/

Flashback: Democrats Worked Hard to Disqualify Overseas Military Ballots in 2000 Recount. 2012, August 6. Retrieved November 15, 2014, from http://www.breitbart.com/Big-Government/2012/08/05/flashback-dems-disqualified-military-ballots-in-2000

Professor Fails Student for Refusing to Conform to His Anti-Christian Bias - Breitbart. 2015, May 6. Retrieved June 10, 2015, from http://www.breitbart.com/big-government/2015/05/06/professor-fails-student-for-refusing-to-conform-to-his-anti-christian-bias/

Bump, P. President Obama's executive orders on guns should be pretty popular. 2016. Retrieved January 07, 2016, from https://www. washingtonpost.com/news/the-fix/wp/2016/01/05/president-obamas-executive-orders-on-guns-are-very-popular-even-if-he-isnt/

CAMERA: Middle East Issues. 2011, September 22. Retrieved November 23, 2014, from http://www.camera.org/index. asp?x_context=7&x_issue=83&x_article=2116

Tallying the Health Care Bill's Giveaways. 2009, December 21. Retrieved November 19, 2014, from http://www.cbsnews.com/news/tallying-the-health-care-bills-giveaways/

Joe Sestak Was Contacted by Bill Clinton About Dropping Primary Bid. 2010, May 28. Retrieved November 19, 2014, from http://www.cbsnews.com/news/joe-sestak-was-contacted-by-bill-clinton-about-dropping-primary-bid/

US to Use Foreign Aid to Promote Gay Rights. 2011, December 6. Retrieved November 24, 2014, from http://www.cbsnews.com/news/us-to-use-foreign-aid-to-promote-gay-rights/

Obama, Dems Wrong to Kill School Vouchers. 2009, March 11. Retrieved November 15, 2014, from http://www.cnn.com/2009/POLITICS/03/11/martin.vouchers/index.html?_s=PM:POLITICS

US Shares Blame for Mexico Drug Violence, Clinton says. 2009, March 26. Retrieved November 18, 2014, from http://www.cnn.com/2009/POLITICS/03/25/clinton.mexico/index.html?eref=ib_us

Osteens: Obama Doing Great Job, Loves the Lord. 2009, April 8. Retrieved November 25, 2014, from http://www.cnn.com/2009/POLITICS/04/08/lkl.osteens/

US Sues South Carolina Over Immigration Law. 2011, October 31. Retrieved November 18, 2014, from http://www.cnn.com/2011/10/31/politics/south-carolina-immigration-suit/

Former Deputy Chief of Mission in Libya: US Military Assets Told to Stand Down. 2013, May 7. Retrieved November 19, 2014, from http://www.cnn.com/2013/05/06/politics/benghazi-whistleblower/

Operation Fast and Furious Fast Facts. 2014, November 7. Retrieved November 18, 2014, from http://www.cnn.com/2013/08/27/world/americas/operation-fast-and-furious-fast-facts/

Judge Strikes Down Pennsylvania Voter ID Law, Calls it Burdensome. 2014, January 17. Retrieved November 25, 2014, from http://www.cnn.com/2014/01/17/politics/pennsylvania-voter-id-law/

McCain to Crowd: 'Don't be Scared' of Obama Presidency. 2008, October 11. Retrieved November 20, 2014, from http://politicalticker.blogs.cnn.com/2008/10/11/mccain-to-crowd-dont-be-scared-of-obama-presidency/

Obama Pledges 'Total Equality' for Same-Sex Families. 2008, August 6. Retrieved July 29, 2015, from http://cnsnews.com/news/article/obama-pledges-total-equality-same-sex-families

Abortion Kills More Black Americans Than the Seven Leading Causes of Death Combined, Says CDC Data. 2009, October 22. Retrieved November 14, 2014, from http://cnsnews.com/news/article/abortion-kills-more-black-americans-seven-leading-causes-death-combined-says-cdc-data

Obama Administration Gives $446 Million to ACORN Veteran. 2012, June 12. Retrieved November 18, 2014, from http://capitalresearch.org/2012/06/obama-administration-gives-446-million-to-acorn-veteran/

Alveda King: Abortionist Attorney Playing Race Card Is Shameful. 2013, March 25. Retrieved November 27, 2014, from http://www.charismanews.com/us/38801-alveda-king-abortionist-attorney-playing-race-card-is-shameful

Pew: Evangelicals Stay Strong as Christianity Crumbles in America. 2015, May 11. Retrieved June 10, 2015, from http://www.

christianitytoday.com/gleanings/2015/may/pew-evangelicals-stay-strong-us-religious-landscape-study.html

Supreme Court Upholds American Flag Ban--for Cinco de Mayo. 2015, April 8. Retrieved June 7, 2015, from http://www.citizen-action.com/supreme-court-upholds-american-flag-ban-cinco-de-mayo/article1011

Civil Rights: Dems Controlled Everything But Would Not Pass Civil Rights: The History The Timeline. 2012, August 19. Retrieved November 27, 2014, from http://www.freerepublic.com/focus/bloggers/2920349/posts

Clinton: Obama Will Ignore Congress on Libya War. 2011, April 1. Retrieved November 18, 2014, from http://www.thenewamerican.com/usnews/constitution/item/7936-clinton-obama-will-ignore-congress-on-libya-war

Coach is Right. 2014, October 12. Retrieved November 25, 2014, from http://www.coachisright.com/ugly-history-democrat-party-part-ten/

Elder: Where are Al Sharpton... 2012, March 15. Retrieved November 16, 2014, from http://www.gopusa.com/commentary/2012/03/15/elder-where-are-al-sharptons-apologies/

Turkey's New. 2015. Retrieved July 29, 2015, from http://www.commondreams.org/views/2015/07/26/turkeys-new-war-terror-mainly-targeting-kurds

Name-Calling: The Favored Weapon of Gay Marriage Supporters - Crisis Magazine. 2012, August 1. Retrieved from http://www.crisismagazine.com/2012/name-calling-the-favored-weapon-of-gay-marriage-supporters

Gay Persecution of Christians: The Latest Evidence - Crisis Magazine. 2013, October 10. Retrieved November 24, 2014, from http://www.crisismagazine.com/2013/gay-persecution-of-christians-the-latest-evidence

Obama Said Americans Safe from ISIS-Style Attack -- While Police Hunted San Bernardino Terrorists! 2015, December 3. Retrieved December 30, 2015, from http://www.dailywire.com/news/1585/obama-said-americans-safe-isis-style-attack-while-ben-shapiro

St. Louis Erupts When Cops Shoot a Criminal, but What About the 9 yr old Killed 24 hours before? * DC Gazette. 2015, August 20. Retrieved November 11, 2015, from http://dcgazette.com/in-st-louis-but-what-happened-when-thugs-killed-a-9-yr-old-24-hours-before/#

Benghazi Timeline. 2014, May 2. Retrieved November 19, 2014, from http://www.factcheck.org/2012/10/benghazi-timeline/

U.N. Agreement Should Have All Gun Owners Up In Arms. 2011, June 7. Retrieved November 19, 2014, from http://www.forbes.com/sites/larrybell/2011/06/07/u-n-agreement-should-have-all-gun-owners-up-in-arms/

Why the Fuss? Obama Has Long Been On Record In Favor Of Redistribution. 2012. Retrieved July 29, 2015, from http://www.forbes.com/sites/paulroderickgregory/2012/09/23/why-the-fuss-obama-has-long-been-on-record-in-favor-of-redistribution/

New Obama Terror Czar To Target Conservatives, Christians – Four States News. 2015, October 21. Retrieved December 31, 2015, from https://www.fourstatesnews.us/2015/10/21/new-obama-terror-czar-to-target-conservatives-christians/

Debt Ceiling Skyrockets, Obama No Longer Calls Bush 'Unpatriotic' for Increases. 2012, January 30. Retrieved November 18, 2014, from http://www.foxnews.com/politics/2012/01/30/as-debt-ceiling-skyrockets-obama-no-longer-calling-bush-increases-unpatriotic/

Supreme Court Upholds ObamaCare Subsidies. 2015, June 25. Retrieved July 29, 2015, from http://www.foxnews.com/politics/2015/06/25/supreme-court-upholds-obamacare-subsidies/

Hillary Goes Ugly Early with Racism Claims. 2015, June 5. Retrieved July 30, 2015, from http://www.foxnews.com/politics/2015/06/05/hillary-goes-ugly-early-with-racism-claims/?intcmp=obinsite

1 in 3 Freed Gitmo Detainees Go Back to Fight; UBL's Former Cook the Latest. 2015. Retrieved December 31, 2015, from http://insider.foxnews.com/2015/12/10/us-intelligence-experts-1-3-guantanamo-bay-detainees-return-terrorism

Contrast Barack Obama's Quotes About Islam With His Quotes About Christianity. 2013, September 28. Retrieved November 20, 2014, from http://freedomoutpost.com/2013/09/contrast-barack-obamas-quotes-islam-quotes-christianity/

Obama Tells People Not to Divide and Discriminate While Doing Just That - Freedom Outpost. 2015, June 5. Retrieved June 7, 2015, from http://freedomoutpost.com/2015/06/obama-tells-people-not-to-divide-and-discriminate-while-doing-just-that/

Anti-Theists Wanting to Court-Martial Air Force General for Speaking About God Don't Get Their Way - Freedom Outpost. 2015, May 24. Retrieved June 10, 2015, from http://freedomoutpost.com/2015/05/anti-theists-wanting-to-court-martial-air-force-general-for-speaking-about-god-doesnt-get-its-way/

Obama: Church Shouldn't Focus Too Much on Protecting the Unborn & Marriage - Freedom Outpost. 2015, May 23. Retrieved June 10, 2015, from http://freedomoutpost.com/2015/05/obama-church-shouldnt-focus-too-much-on-protecting-the-unborn-marriage/

National Black Republican Association. 2009. Retrieved November 25, 2014, from http://www.nationalblackrepublicans.com/FrequentlyAskedQuestions#Slavery:__Democrats_Fought_to_Expand_It___Republicans_Fought_to_End_It

Obama's Czars and Their Left-Wing Affiliations. 2011, May 16. Retrieved November 19, 2014, from http://www.frontpagemag.com/2011/mike-bauer/obama's-czars-and-their-left-wing-affiliations/

Assisted Suicide: A Retreat to the 1967 Borders. 2011, August 4. Retrieved November 23, 2014, from http://www.frontpagemag.com/2011/charles-bybelezer/assisted-suicide-a-retreat-to-the-1967-borders/

Operation Fast and Furious and the Massacre of Mexican Kids. 2012, October 2. Retrieved November 18, 2014, from http://www.frontpagemag.com/2012/joseph-klein/operation-fast-and-furious-and-the-massacre-of-mexican-kids/

Obama: The Most-Racial President. 2012, May 11. Retrieved November 25, 2014, from http://www.frontpagemag.com/2012/mark-tapson/obama-the-most-racial-president/

John Kerry's Blackmail. 2014, February 3. Retrieved November 23, 2014, from http://www.frontpagemag.com/2014/ronn-torossian/john-kerrys-blackmail/

Obama Signs Iran Deal as Rouhani Attends a 'Death to America' Event. 2015, July 15. Retrieved July 29, 2015, from http://

www.frontpagemag.com/fpm/259471/obama-signs-iran-deal-rouhani-attends-death-ari-lieberman

"Pro-Life" Pennsylvania Senator Bob Casey: I Will Oppose Bill to De-Fund Planned Parenthood. 2015. Retrieved July 30, 2015, from http://www.lifenews.com/2015/07/29/pro-life-pennsylvania-senator-bob-casey-i-will-oppose-bill-to-de-fund-planned-parenthood/

Report: Obama Told NSC and FBI To 'Downplay' Terrorist Angle Of San Bernardino | Georgia News Network. 2015. Retrieved December 30, 2015, from http://www.georgianewsnetwork. com/articles/national-news-104668/report-obama-told-nsc-and-fbi-14195602/

Obama Attempts to Suppress Ohio Military Vote. 2012, August 6. Retrieved November 15, 2014, from http://news.investors. com/ibd-editorials/080612-621176-democrats-seek-to-restrict-military-voting.htm?p=full

J. R. Maroney Blog. 2012. Retrieved November 12, 2015, from http://www.jrmaroney.com/why-bill-clinton-is-responsible-for-north-koreas-successful-missile-program/

Black Panther Boss Who Got Off for Voter Intimidation Arrested - Judicial Watch. 2013, June 28. Retrieved November 18, 2014, from http://www.judicialwatch.org/blog/2013/06/black-panther-boss-who-got-off-for-voter-intimidation-arrested/

JESSE JACKSON EXPOSED. 2006. Retrieved November 15, 2014, from http://www.judicialwatch.org/archive/2006/ jackson-report.pdf

Learning from History Famous Quotations and Quotes. n.d.. Retrieved November 16, 2014, from http://www.age-of-the-sage.org/philosophy/history/learning_from_history.html

Black Religious Leaders Wrongly Giddy Over Pro-Abortion Barack Obama. 2008, June 10. Retrieved November 25, 2014, from http://www.lifenews.com/2008/06/10/nat-3968/

Massive Fraud Case Against Planned Parenthood Moving Forward. 2011, August 3. Retrieved November 14, 2014, from http://www.lifenews.com/2011/08/03/massive-fraud-case-against-planned-parenthood-moving-forward/

Phill Kline: Sebelius Worked to Protect Planned Parenthood. 2011, November 10. Retrieved November 18, 2014, from http://www.lifenews.com/2011/11/10/phill-kline-sebelius-worked-to-protect-planned-parenthood/

Obama Admin Pushes Sex on Kids, Children are "Sexual Beings". 2011, August 23. Retrieved November 24, 2014, from http://www.lifenews.com/2011/08/23/obama-admin-pushes-sex-on-kids-children-are-sexual-beings/

Forget Akin, Obama Ignored Planned Parenthood Sex Trafficking Videos. 2012, August 23. Retrieved November 14, 2014, from http://www.lifenews.com/2012/08/23/forget-akin-obama-ignored-planned-parenthood-sex-trafficking-videos/

Abortion Methods and Abortion Procedures Used to Kill Unborn Babies. 2013, January 2. Retrieved November 14, 2014, from http://www.lifenews.com/2013/01/02/abortion-methods-and-abortion-procedures-used-to-kill-unborn-babies/

NAACP President Quits, Turned Civil Rights Org Into Pro-Abortion Group. 2013, September 9. Retrieved November 15, 2014, from http://www.lifenews.com/2013/09/09/naacp-president-resigns-turned-civil-rights-org-into-pro-abortion-group/

Planned Parenthood Has More African-American Blood on Its Hands Than the KKK. 2013, June 7. Retrieved November 27,

2014, from http://www.lifenews.com/2013/06/07/planned-parenthood-has-more-african-american-blood-on-its-hands-than-the-kkk/

Hillary Clinton: I Admire Planned Parenthood Founder Margaret Sanger. 2014. Retrieved July 30, 2015, from http://www.lifenews.com/2014/09/23/hillary-clinton-i-admire-planned-parenthood-founder-margaret-sanger/

This Isn't the First Time Planned Parenthood Sold Aborted Baby Parts, See What it Did 17 Years Ago. 2015. Retrieved July 30, 2015, from http://www.lifenews.com/2015/07/23/this-isnt-the-first-time-planned-parenthood-sold-aborted-baby-parts-see-what-it-did-17-years-ago/

Hillary Clinton on Planned Parenthood Selling Aborted Babies: "They Do Really Good Work". 2015. Retrieved July 30, 2015, from http://www.lifenews.com/2015/07/29/hillary-clinton-on-planned-parenthood-selling-aborted-babies-they-do-really-good-work/

Democrats Promise to Kill Bill De-Funding Planned Parenthood; Harry Reid: "Good Luck With That". 2015. Retrieved July 30, 2015, from http://www.lifenews.com/2015/07/28/democrats-promise-to-kill-bill-de-funding-planned-parenthood-harry-reid-good-luck-with-that/

Planned Parenthood - Racist Donations Welcome We Abort Black Babies. 2008, April 3. Retrieved November 14, 2014, from https://www.lifesitenews.com/news/planned-parenthood-racist-donations-welcome-we-abort-black-babies

Obama Declares He Doesn't Want His Children "Punished with a Baby". 2008, April 1. Retrieved November 25, 2014, from https://www.lifesitenews.com/news/obama-declares-he-doesnt-want-his-children-punished-with-a-baby

Another Undercover Video Shows Kentucky Abortuary Failing to Report Child Sex Abuse. 2010, April 21. Retrieved November 14, 2014, from https://www.lifesitenews.com/news/another-undercover-video-shows-kentucky-abortuary-failing-to-report-child-s

Hillary Clinton: 'Religious Beliefs' Against Abortion 'Have to be Changed'. 2015, April 24. Retrieved June 10, 2015, from https://www.lifesitenews.com/news/hillary-clinton-religious-beliefs-that-oppose-abortion-have-to-be-changed

NOW President: Babies Wouldn't Die So Much If We'd Just Kill Them Before They Died! 2015, May 14. Retrieved June 10, 2015, from https://www.lifesitenews.com/blogs/now-president-babies-wouldnt-die-so-much-if-wed-just-kill-them-before-they

Black Clergy Tackle Homophobia. 2006, January 21. Retrieved November 16, 2014, from http://articles.latimes.com/2006/jan/21/nation/na-clergy21

Keystone XL Pipeline Decision Delayed Until After 2012 Election. 2011, November 11. Retrieved November 18, 2014, from http://articles.latimes.com/2011/nov/11/nation/la-na-keystone-20111111

Frank Lombard Duke University Professor Rapes and Video Taped African-American Adopted Son Sentenced to 27 years. 2012, October 31. Retrieved November 15, 2014, from http://ressurrection.wordpress.com/2012/10/31/frank-lombard-duke-university-professor-rapes-and-video-taped-african-american-adopted-son-sentenced-to-27-years/

Peter Lucas: Will Deserter Bergdahl Get a Rose Garden Pardon? 2015, April 1. Retrieved June 7, 2015, from http://www.

lowellsun.com/peterlucas/ci_27819174/peter-lucas-will-deserter-bergdahl-get-rose-garden

NAACP Presents Case Against US Voter ID Laws to United Nations. 2013, March 16. Retrieved November 15, 2014, from http://www.mrctv.org/blog/naacp-presents-case-against-us-voter-id-laws-united-nations

10 Scandals Involving Hillary Clinton You May Have Forgotten. 2015, March 10. Retrieved June 7, 2015, from http://www.mrctv.org/blog/10-scandals-involving-hillary-clinton-you-may-have-forgotten

As Violence Spikes in Some Cities, Is 'Ferguson Effect' to Blame? 2015, June 2. Retrieved June 4, 2015, from http://www.nbcnews.com/news/us-news/violence-spikes-some-cities-ferguson-effect-blame-n368526

Christians In US On Decline As Number Of 'Nones' Grows, Survey Finds. 2015, May 12. Retrieved June 10, 2015, from http://www.npr.org/sections/thetwo-way/2015/05/12/406154155/christians-in-u-s-on-decline-as-number-of-nones-grows-survey-finds

Rosenbaum and Abraham: Sharpton's True Role in Crown Heights. 2011, August 24. Retrieved November 16, 2014, from http://www.nydailynews.com/opinion/al-sharpton-true-role-crown-heights-yankel-rosenbaum-brother-speaks-article-1.945812

Sen. Byrd Questions Obama's Use of Policy 'Czars' 2009, February 25. Retrieved November 19, 2014, from http://www.nytimes.com/gwire/2009/02/25/25greenwire-byrd-questions-obamas-use-of-policy-czars-9865.html

How to Respond to Dan Savage on Homosexuality and the Bible? 2012, April 29. Retrieved November 19, 2014, from http://

www.ncregister.com/blog/jimmy-akin/how-to-respond-to-dan-savage-on-homosexuality-and-the-bible

Andrew C. McCarthy - Why Does Interpol Need Immunity from American Law? 2009, December 23. Retrieved November 19, 2014, from http://www.nationalreview.com/corner/191918/why-does-interpol-need-immunity-american-law-andrew-c-mccarthy

Andrew C. McCarthy - Who Are the Gitmo 9? 2010, February 24. Retrieved November 19, 2014, from http://www.nationalreview.com/corner/195357/who-are-gitmo-9-andrew-c-mccarthy

Peter Kirsanow - Blacks, Democrats, and Republicans. 2011, March 15. Retrieved November 25, 2014, from http://www.nationalreview.com/corner/262180/blacks-democrats-and-republicans-peter-kirsanow

Peter Kirsanow - Clarifying Obama's Vote On Born-Alive. 2012, February 10. Retrieved November 14, 2014, from http://www.nationalreview.com/corner/290764/clarifying-obamas-vote-born-alive-peter-kirsanow

Roger Clegg - Latest Statistics on Illegitimate Births. 2012, October 4. Retrieved November 14, 2014, from http://www.nationalreview.com/corner/329432/latest-statistics-illegitimate-births-roger-clegg

Deroy Murdock - Remember Fast and Furious's Mexican Victims. 2012, July 6. Retrieved November 19, 2014, from http://www.nationalreview.com/articles/304835/remember-fast-and-furious-s-mexican-victims-deroy-murdock

Kevin D. Williamson - The Party of Civil Rights. 2012, May 28. Retrieved November 27, 2014, from http://www.

nationalreview.com/articles/300432/party-civil-rights-kevin-d-williamson/page/0/3

Victor Davis Hanson - The Obama Borg. 2013, April 30. Retrieved November 20, 2014, from http://www.nationalreview.com/article/346930/obama-borg

Obama: Transforming America. 2013. Retrieved July 29, 2015, from http://www.nationalreview.com/article/359967/obama-transforming-america-victor-davis-hanson

The O Jesse Knows. 2008, October 14. Retrieved November 22, 2014, from http://nypost.com/2008/10/14/the-o-jesse-knows/

Yes, Hillary Clinton Broke the Law. 2015. Retrieved November 11, 2015, from http://nypost.com/2015/09/27/yes-hillary-clinton-broke-the-law/?utm_source=zergnet.com&utm_medium=referral&utm_campaign=zergnet_710858

UPDATE: Rev. Al Sharpton's Official Statement On Arizona Immigration Law. 2010, April 26. Retrieved November 15, 2014, from http://newsone.com/495492/sharpton-compares-ariz-immigration-law-to-apartheid-nazi-germany/

CNN Brings on Al Sharpton to Forward Idea that Rangel Probe Is Racially Motivated. 2010, August 2. Retrieved November 16, 2014, from http://newsbusters.org/blogs/matthew-balan/2010/08/02/cnns-lemon-forwards-idea-rangel-investigation-racially-motivated

Krauthammer Rips Obama on America's Global Standing; 'You Wonder...What Planet He's Living on' 2015. Retrieved June 3, 2015, from http://newsbusters.org/blogs/curtis-houck/2015/06/02/krauthammer-rips-obama-americas-global-standing-you-wonderwhat-planet

NewsMax. Report: Gun Prosecution Cases Plunge Under Obama. 2014. Retrieved January 10, 2016, from http://www.newsmax. com/US/gun-prosecutions-Obama-decline/2014/07/24/ id/584608/

Obama Puts Blame on Bush, Iraq War for Rise of ISIS. 2015, March 17. Retrieved June 7, 2015, from http://www.newsmax. com/Newsfront/iraq-isis-george-w-bush-obama/2015/03/17/ id/630545/

'Obamacare Architect's' Emails Show Close Ties With WH: WSJ. 2015, June 22. Retrieved July 29, 2015, from http://www. newsmax.com/newswidget/Jonathan-Gruber-obamacare-emails-HHS/2015/06/22/id/651615/?Dkt_nbr=F6A9-1&nmx_source=Trib_Live&nmx_medium=widget&nmx_content=439&nmx_campaign=widgetphase2

13 Shocking Revelations from Hillary's Benghazi Hearing. 2015, October 23. Retrieved November 12, 2015, from http://www. newsmax.com/TheWire/hillary-clinton-benghazi-hearing-revelations/2015/10/23/id/697712/

Bergdahl: Taliban Captors Asked Me Often About Life in America. 2015, December 25. Retrieved December 29, 2015, from http:// www.newsmax.com/Newsfront/bergdahl-taliban-obama-gay/2015/12/25/id/707079/?ns_mail_uid=936716&ns_mail_job=1647557_12252015&s=al&dkt_nbr=98b9vbot

Franklin Graham: 'I Have Resigned from the Republican Party' 2015, December 22. Retrieved December 29, 2015, from http://www.newsmax.com/Newsfront/franklin-graham-resigns-the/2015/12/22/id/706826/

Obama's Never-Ending Defense of Islam Ensures More Bombing Attacks. 2013, April 22. Retrieved December 30, 2015, from http://www.nowtheendbegins.com/obamas-never-ending-defense-of-islam-ensures-more-bombing-attacks/

Obama Blocked Born-Alive Infant Protection Act | CitizenLink. 2008, April 2. Retrieved November 25, 2014, from http://www.citizenlink.com/2008/04/02/citizenlink-obama-blocked-born-alive-infant-protection-act/

Fact Sheet: Outcomes for Young, Black Men. 2014. Retrieved November 17, 2014, from http://www.pbs.org/wnet/tavissmiley/tsr/too-important-to-fail/fact-sheet-outcomes-for-young-black-men/

Obama "Terrorizing" Aurora Killings but Fort Hood Jihad is "Workplace Violence". 2012, July 30. Retrieved November 20, 2014, from http://pamelageller.com/2012/07/obamas-comments-on-aurora-killer-and-the-islamic-attack-at-ft-hood.html/

A Religious Portrait of African-Americans. 2009, January 30. Retrieved November 25, 2014, from http://www.pewforum.org/2009/01/30/a-religious-portrait-of-african-americans/

[VIDEO]Lie of the Year: 'If You Like Your Health Care Plan, You Can Keep It' 2013, November 12. Retrieved November 21, 2014, from http://www.politifact.com/truth-o-meter/article/2013/dec/12/lie-year-if-you-like-your-health-care-plan-keep-it/

Bill of Lies: A History of Obamacare. 2015. Retrieved July 29, 2015, from http://politicalbeacon.com/HERE/bill-of-lies-a-history-of-obamacare/

Reconstruction1. n.d. Retrieved November 27, 2014, from http://whgbetc.com/mind/reconstruction1.html

Palestinians Deploy Obama Speech in U.N. Campaign. 2011, September 7. Retrieved November 23, 2014, from http://www.

reuters.com/article/2011/09/07/us-palestinians-israel-obama-idUSTRE7861LN20110907

Demographics. 2013. Retrieved March 7, 2015, from http://srmo. sagepub.com/view/encyc-of-research-design/n108.xml

Lindsey Graham's War Lie: Bigger than Richard Blumenthal's. 2010, May 20. Retrieved November 21, 2014, from http://www. salon.com/2010/05/20/lindsey_graham_war_liar/

Samuel Adams Quotes. 2015. Retrieved July 29, 2015, from http:// www.goodreads.com/author/quotes/31693.Samuel_Adams

LGBT Leaders to Attend White House Reception Honoring Pride Month. 2011, June 29. Retrieved November 24, 2014, from http://sdgln.com/news/2011/06/29/lgbt-leaders-attend-white-house-reception-honoring-pride-month#sthash.xKUdN9j2. dpbs

When the Tide Turned in the Civil War. 2013, July 18. Retrieved November 27, 2014, from http://socialistworker. org/2013/07/18/the-tide-turns-in-the-civil-war

Jesse Shakedown Jackson Gets Beer Distributorship for Son. 2001, April 8. Retrieved November 15, 2014, from http://solargeneral. org/wp-content/uploads/library/Black-Civil-Wrongs/jesse-shakedown-jackson-gets-beer-distributorship-for-son.pdf

Obama's Gay Marriage Conundrum | TIME.com. 2012, May 8. Retrieved November 24, 2014, from http://swampland.time. com/2012/05/08/obamas-gay-marriage-conundrum/

Top Moments in Politicians Lying About Military Service. 2010, May 31. Retrieved November 21, 2014, from http:// talkingpointsmemo.com/dc/top-moments-in-politicians-lying-about-military-service

The Black Codes. n.d. Retrieved November 27, 2014, from http://history-world.org/black_codes.htm

In Diversity We Trust? Obama Botches US National Motto. 2010, December 6. Retrieved November 21, 2014, from http://www.theblaze.com/stories/2010/12/06/in-diversity-we-trust-obama-botches-u-s-national-motto/

Powell Endorses Obama. 2008, October 19. Retrieved November 25, 2014, from http://thecaucus.blogs.nytimes.com/2008/10/19/powell-endorses-obama/?_r=0

Democratic Mischief: Liberal Voters Turn Out in Attempt to Topple Romney in Michigan. 2012, February 28. Retrieved November 20, 2014, from http://www.thedailybeast.com/articles/2012/02/28/michigan-s-primary-party-crashers-democrats-crossing-over-to-thwart-romney.html

Why Does the NAACP Support Abortion? 2011, December 23. Retrieved November 15, 2014, from http://dailycaller.com/2011/12/23/why-does-the-naacp-support-abortion/

Homeland Security Guidelines Advise Deference to Pro-Shariah Muslim Supremacists. 2013, May 17. Retrieved November 20, 2014, from http://dailycaller.com/2013/05/17/homeland-security-guidelines-advise-deference-to-pro-sharia-muslim-supremacists/

The Democrat Party's Long and Shameful History of Bigotry and Racism. 2001. Retrieved November 27, 2014, from http://gopcapitalist.tripod.com/democratrecord.html

Ninth Circuit Affirms Schools Can Ban Shirts with US Flags on Them to Avoid Upsetting Mexican Students. n.d. Retrieved November 18, 2014, from http://www.thefederalistpapers.org/us/ninth-circuit-affirms-schools-can-ban-shirts-with-u-s-flags-on-them-to-avoid-upsetting-mexican-students

Eric Holder's Radical Far Left Attorney Claimed Khalid Sheikh Mohammad Was Tortured; Pushed to Throw Out His Guilty Plea. 2010, February 23. Retrieved November 19, 2014, from http://www.thegatewaypundit.com/2010/02/eric-holders-radical-pro-terrorist-attorney-claims-khalid-sheikh-mohammad-was-tortured-wants-his-guilty-plea-thrown-out/comment-page-2/

An Executive Unbound: The Obama Administration's Unilateral Actions. 2014, February 12. Retrieved November 21, 2014, from http://www.heritage.org/research/reports/2014/02/an-executive-unbound-the-obama-administrations-unilateral-actions

Eric Holder "More Deeply Involved" In Rich Pardon Than Supporters Acknowledge. 2008, December 1. Retrieved November 19, 2014, from http://www.huffingtonpost.com/2008/12/01/nyt-holder-more-deeply-in_n_147605.html

Should We Want Movies Like Sandra Bullock's *The Blind Side?* 2009, September 21. Retrieved November 27, 2014, from http://www.huffingtonpost.com/mark-blankenship/should-we-want-movies-lik_b_293888.html

Leon Panetta, US Defense Secretary, Urges Israel to 'Just Get To The Damned Table' 2011, December 3. Retrieved November 23, 2014, from http://www.huffingtonpost.com/2011/12/03/leon-panetta-israel_n_1127133.html

Black, Latino Students Perform at Levels of 30 Years Ago. 2012, January 23. Retrieved November 15, 2014, from http://www.huffingtonpost.com/2012/01/23/black-latino-students-per_n_1224790.html

GOP Pollster gets 'Wobbly' from Listening to Trump Supporters. The Loft -- GOPUSA. 2015. Retrieved November 11, 2015, from http://www.gopusa.com/theloft/2015/08/26/gop-pollster-gets-wobbly-from-listening-to-trump-supporters/

Clinton Says Chinese Money Did Not Influence US Policy. 1998, May 17. Retrieved November 12, 2015, from http://www.nytimes.com/1998/05/18/us/clinton-says-chinese-money-did-not-influence-us-policy.html

A Host Disparages Obama, and McCain Quickly Apologizes. 2008, February 26. Retrieved November 20, 2014, from http://www.nytimes.com/2008/02/27/us/politics/27name.html

Candidate's Words on Vietnam Service Differ from History. 2010, May 17. Retrieved November 21, 2014, from http://www.nytimes.com/2010/05/18/nyregion/18blumenthal.html?pagewanted=all&_r=0

Man Behind Anti-Islam Video Gets Prison Term. 2012, November 7. Retrieved November 20, 2014, from http://www.nytimes.com/2012/11/08/us/maker-of-anti-islam-video-gets-prison-term.html?_r=0

Obama Says Same-Sex Marriage Should Be Legal. 2012, May 9. Retrieved November 24, 2014, from http://www.nytimes.com/2012/05/10/us/politics/obama-says-same-sex-marriage-should-be-legal.html?pagewanted=all&_r=0

Don't Dare Call the Health Law 'Redistribution'. 2013, November 23. Retrieved July 29, 2015, from http://www.nytimes.com/2013/11/24/us/dont-dare-call-the-health-law-redistribution.html?_r=0

Report Finds Hispanics Faring Better Than Blacks. 2014, April 2. Retrieved November 17, 2014, from http://www.nytimes.com/2014/04/03/us/report-finds-hispanics-faring-better-than-blacks.html?_r=2

Supreme Court Allows Nationwide Health Care Subsidies. 2015, June 25. Retrieved July 29, 2015, from http://www.nytimes. com/2015/06/26/us/obamacare-supreme-court.html

Boy Scouts' President Calls for End to Ban on Gay Leaders. 2015, May 21. Retrieved July 29, 2015, from http://www.nytimes. com/2015/05/22/us/boy-scouts-president-calls-for-end-to-ban-on-gay-leaders.html?_r=2

Cash Flowed to Clinton Foundation Amid Russian Uranium Deal. 2015, April 23. Retrieved November 12, 2015, from http:// www.nytimes.com/2015/04/24/us/cash-flowed-to-clinton-foundation-as-russians-pressed-for-control-of-uranium-company.html?_r=2

Holder's Black Panther Stonewall. 2009, August 9. Retrieved November 27, 2014, from http://online.wsj.com/news/articles/ SB10001424052970203550604574361071968458430

Jesse Jackson: 'You Can't Vote Against Healthcare and Call Yourself a Black Man' 2009, November 18. Retrieved November 15, 2014, from http://thehill.com/homenews/house/68451-jackson-you-cant-vote-against-healthcare-and-call-yourself-a-black-man

Senate Women Threaten Shutdown Over Planned Parenthood Rider. 2011, April 8. Retrieved November 27, 2014, from http://thehill.com/homenews/senate/154939-senate-women-threaten-shutdwown-over-planned-parenthood-rider

UN Backs Iran Deal, Infuriating Lawmakers from Both Parties. 2015, July 20. Retrieved July 30, 2015, from http://thehill. com/homenews/administration/248589-un-backs-iran-deal-infuriating-lawmakers

Obama: Climate Summit a 'Powerful Rebuke' to Terrorists. 2015, November 24. Retrieved December 30, 2015, from http://

thehill.com/policy/energy-environment/261193-obama-climate-conference-is-powerful-rebuke-to-terrorists

TIMELINE: Tracking Barack Obama's Position On Marriage Equality. 2011, June 22. Retrieved November 24, 2014, from http://thinkprogress.org/lgbt/2011/06/22/250931/timeline-barack-obama-marriage-equality/

Elizabeth Warren Is Rewriting History. 2014, April 22. Retrieved November 21, 2014, from http://www.usnews.com/opinion/blogs/brian-walsh/2014/04/22/elizabeth-warren-glosses-over-native-american-controversy-in-new-book

House Panel Votes to Cite Holder for Contempt of Congress. 2012, May 21. Retrieved November 19, 2014, from http://usatoday30.usatoday.com/news/washington/story/2012-06-20/holder-contempt-House-vote/55717644/1

Unruh, B. McCain Calls for Answer to Cruz's White House Eligibility. 2016. Retrieved January 10, 2016, from http://www.wnd.com/2016/01/mccain-calls-for-answer-to-cruz-white-house-eligibility/

W.E.B. Du Bois, "The Talented Tenth" n.d. Retrieved November 14, 2014, from http://www.yale.edu/glc/archive/1148.htm

Is Declaration of Independence Unconstitutional? 2004, November 23. Retrieved November 18, 2014, from http://www.wnd.com/2004/11/27718/

Dodd Has Explaining to Do. 2004, April 14. Retrieved November 27, 2014, from http://www.wnd.com/2004/04/24168/

Abortion Hitting Social Security Hard. 2005, February 16. Retrieved November 14, 2014, from http://www.wnd.com/2005/02/28936/

Clinton Blood Scandal Exposed in New Film. 2005. Retrieved November 12, 2015, from http://www.wnd.com/2005/10/33137/

Why Black Republicans Support Obama. 2008. Retrieved November 25, 2014, from http://www.wnd.com/2008/07/68779/

Obama Science Czar Holdren Called for Forced Abortions. 2009, July 7. Retrieved November 14, 2014, from http://www.wnd.com/2009/07/103707/

Homeland Security on Guard for 'Right-Wing Extremists'. 2009. Retrieved December 31, 2015, from http://www.wnd.com/2009/04/94803/

Investigation of 'Antiwhite Bias' Grows. 2010, July 6. Retrieved November 27, 2014, from http://www.wnd.com/2010/07/175729/

Obama Adviser: American Freedom, Equality Are Just 'Myths'. 2011, May 4. Retrieved November 19, 2014, from http://www.wnd.com/2011/05/294821/

Congress Backtracks on Plan to Legalize Bestiality. 2011, December 13. Retrieved November 24, 2014, from http://www.wnd.com/2011/12/377233/

Why the Surprise About Push for 'Pedophile Rights'? 2011, August 28. Retrieved November 24, 2014, from http://www.wnd.com/2011/08/338921/

The Godless Democrats. 2012, September 7. Retrieved November 20, 2014, from http://www.wnd.com/2012/09/the-godless-democrats/

Most 'Biblically Hostile' President Ever is .... 2012, March 11. Retrieved November 21, 2014, from http://www.wnd.com/2012/03/most-biblically-hostile-president-ever-is/

Claim: Obama Hid 'Gay Life' to Become President. 2012, September 11. Retrieved November 24, 2014, from http://www.wnd.com/2012/09/claim-obama-hid-gay-life-to-become-president/

Obama Takes Swipe at Christians — Again! 2015, April 7. Retrieved June 7, 2015, from http://www.wnd.com/2015/04/obama-takes-swipe-at-christians-again/

Now It's Biden vs. Bible on Homosexuality. 2015, May 20. Retrieved June 10, 2015, from http://www.wnd.com/2015/05/now-its-biden-vs-bible-on-homosexuality/

Pelosi Wants Planned Parenthood Investigators ... Investigated! 2015. Retrieved July 30, 2015, from http://www.wnd.com/2015/07/pelosi-wants-planned-parenthood-investigators-investigated/#TvFjOqgFhzixaA3q.99

Shooter's Motive Stumps Obama, FBI, Media. 2015. Retrieved July 30, 2015, from http://www.wnd.com/2015/07/shooters-motive-stumps-obama-fbi-media/

Kerry Bombshell: U.N. in 'Secret Deal' with Iran. 2015. Retrieved July 30, 2015, from http://www.wnd.com/2015/07/kerry-bombshell-u-n-in-secret-deal-with-iran/

ISIS Smuggler: 'We Will Use Refugee Crisis to Infiltrate West'. 2015. Retrieved December 30, 2015, from http://www.wnd.com/2015/09/isis-smuggler-we-will-use-refugee-crisis-to-infiltrate-west/

Priebus and Ryan Curtsy to Muslims. 2015. Retrieved December 30, 2015, from http://www.wnd.com/2015/12/priebus-and-ryan-curtsy-to-muslims/

Kenya Gives Obama Abortion, Islamic Courts. 2010, August 5. Retrieved November 18, 2014, from http://www.wnd.com/2010/08/187877/

Radicals Attack US Embassy, Obama Apologizes. Will Romney Speak Out? UPDATE: Romney speaks out | WashingtonExaminer. com. 2012, September 11. Retrieved November 20, 2014, from http://www.washingtonexaminer.com/radicals-attack-us-embassy-obama-apologizes.-will-romney-speak-out-update-romney-speaks-out/article/2507674

Holder to Brief Black Pastors on Campaign 2012 | WashingtonExaminer.com. 2012, May 29. Retrieved November 25, 2014, from http://www.washingtonexaminer.com/holder-to-brief-black-pastors-on-campaign-2012/article/1317501

Why Obama Still Calls Yemen a Success | WashingtonExaminer. com. 2015, March 26. Retrieved June 7, 2015, from http://www.washingtonexaminer.com/why-obama-still-calls-yemen-a-success/article/2562059

Hamas Refuses to Stop Killing Jews. 2014, May 16. Retrieved November 23, 2014, from http://freebeacon.com/national-security/hamas-refuses-to-stop-killing-jews/

Richard Cohen - Eric Holder Is Disqualified by the Marc Rich Pardon. 2008, December 2. Retrieved November 19, 2014, from http://www.washingtonpost.com/wp-dyn/content/article/2008/12/01/AR2008120102403.html

From Video to Terrorist Attack: A Definitive Timeline of Administration Statements on the Libya Attack. 2012, September 27. Retrieved November 20, 2014, from http://www.washingtonpost.com/blogs/fact-checker/post/from-video-to-terrorist-attack-a-definitive-timeline-of-administration-statements-on-the-libya-attack/2012/09/26/86105782-0826-11e2-afff-d6c7f20a83bf_blog.html

Black Church Leaders Try to Inspire Congregants to Vote for Obama. 2012, September 3. Retrieved November 24,

2014, from http://www.washingtonpost.com/politics/ black-church-leaders-try-to-inspire-congregants-to-vote-for-obama/2012/09/03/136b2da0-f3f0-11e1-892d-bc92fee603a7_story.html

President Barack Obama's Support of Gay Marriage Splits African Americans. 2012, May 25. Retrieved November 24, 2014, from http://www.washingtonpost.com/blogs/therootdc/post/ president-barack-obamas-support-of-gay-marriage-splits-african-americans/2012/05/24/gJQAwWCZnU_blog.html

President Obama and the 'Red Line' on Syria's Chemical Weapons. 2013, September 6. Retrieved November 19, 2014, from http://www.washingtonpost.com/blogs/fact-checker/ wp/2013/09/06/president-obama-and-the-red-line-on-syrias-chemical-weapons/

Ben Carson's Stories of Violence in His Past Questioned. 2015. Retrieved November 12, 2015, from https://www. washingtonpost.com/news/morning-mix/wp/2015/11/06/ ben-carsons-stories-of-violence-in-his-past-questioned/

The Real Judge Charles Pickering. 2004, April 25. Retrieved November 27, 2014, from http://www.washingtontimes.com/ news/2004/apr/25/20040425-102732-4061r/?page=all

Obama to be Prayer Day No-Show. 2009, May 6. Retrieved November 24, 2014, from http://www.washingtontimes.com/ news/2009/may/06/prayer-day-no-show/?page=all

SEDLAK: Planned Parenthood: What About the Fraud? 2011, June 3. Retrieved November 14, 2014, from http://www. washingtontimes.com/news/2011/jun/3/planned-parenthood-what-about-the-fraud/?page=all#pagebreak

NUGENT: Racism Lives at Department of Injustice. 2011, March 14. Retrieved November 14, 2014, from http://www.

washingtontimes.com/news/2011/mar/14/racism-lives-at-department-of-injustice/?page=all

GOP Foiled as Funds Flow to Planned Parenthood. 2012, May 7. Retrieved November 18, 2014, from http://www. washingtontimes.com/news/2012/may/7/gop-foiled-as-funds-flow-to-planned-parenthood/?page=all

Michelle Obama Tells Blacks to Vote Democrat - It's the Right Thing to Do. 2014, November 4. Retrieved November 14, 2014, from http://www.washingtontimes.com/news/2014/nov/4/michelle-obama-tells-blacks-to-vote-democrat-its-t/

BRUCE: Obama's Bizarre Immigration Rules. 2014, March 6. Retrieved November 20, 2014, from http://www. washingtontimes.com/news/2014/mar/6/bruce-obamas-bizarre-immigration-rules/?page=all

Paris Attacks Came Hours After Obama Declared Islamic State 'Contained'. 2015. Retrieved December 30, 2015, from http://www.washingtontimes.com/news/2015/nov/14/paris-attacks-came-hours-after-obama-declared-isla/

The Mystery of Barack Obama Continues | Obama Social Security Numbers. n.d.. Retrieved November 19, 2014, from http://www.westernjournalism.com/exclusive-investigative-reports/the-mystery-of-barack-obama-continues/

Obama Apologizes to Muslims After They Murdered Chris Stevens in Libya!. 2012, September 13. Retrieved November 19, 2014, from http://www.westernjournalism.com/obama-apologizes-to-muslims-after-they-murdered-chris-stevens-in-libya/

Wilde, R. Roger Stone: Hillary Used Threats to Silence Bill's Sexual Assault Victims. 2015. Retrieved January 10, 2016, from http://www.breitbart.com/big-government/2015/09/27/roger-stone-pets-killed-tires-slashed-late-night-phone-calls-to-silence-bill-clintons-sexual-assault-victims/

WorldNet Daily. Release of 36,000 Criminal Illegals Impeachable Offense? 2014. Retrieved January 10, 2016, from http://www.wnd.com/2014/05/release-of-36000-criminal-illegals-impeachable-offense/

Obama's Election and the Campaign Reveals a Deep Racial Divide Within America's Churches. 2008, November 8. Retrieved November 20, 2014, from http://www.cleveland.com/nation/index.ssf/2008/11/obamas_election_and_the_campai.html

How Clinton Sold the US Out to China's Military. 2003, October 6. Retrieved November 19, 2014, from http://www.freerepublic.com/focus/f-news/995809/posts

Obama's Czars with Pictures and goals. 2012, January 24. Retrieved November 19, 2014, from http://www.freerepublic.com/focus/news/2919893/posts

Bush vs. Kerry at a Glance. 2004, September 22. Retrieved November 25, 2014, from http://www.nbcnews.com/id/4448630/ns/politics/t/bush-vs-kerry-glance/#.VHQ6wyx0zmQ

Obama Defends Plan to Build Mosque nNear gGround zZero. 2010, August 14. Retrieved November 17, 2014, from http://www.nbcnews.com/id/38698500/ns/politics-white_house/t/obama-defends-plan-build-mosque-near-ground-zero/#.VGmhpyx0zmQ

US Students lLag in iInternational eEducation rRanking. 2013, December 4. Retrieved November 15, 2014, from http://www.msnbc.com/morning-joe/us-students-lag-global-education-ranking

Democrats Split on Whether to Champion or Condemn Snowden. 2015, October 14. Retrieved November 12, 2015, from http://www.msnbc.com/msnbc/democratic-divisions-over-what-make-edward-snowden

Star Parker - The NAACP's Fight Against Private sSchool vVouchers. 2006, May 15. Retrieved November 15, 2014, from http://townhall.com/columnists/starparker/2006/05/15/the_naacps_fight_against_private_school_vouchers/page/full

FLASHBACK: Al Sharpton's Marchers in New York City Chant "What Do We Want? Dead Cops!" 2014, December 21. Retrieved June 4, 2015, from http://townhall.com/tipsheet/katiepavlich/2014/12/21/flashback-al-sharptons-marchers-in-new-york-city-chant-what-do-we-want-dead-cops-n1934308

FBI: Number of Police Officers Killed On-Duty Up by 89 Percent In 2014. 2015, May 11. Retrieved June 4, 2015, from http://townhall.com/tipsheet/katiepavlich/2015/05/11/fbi-murders-of-police-officers-were-up-in-2014-n1997416

Radical Reconstruction. n.d. Retrieved November 27, 2014, from http://www.ushistory.org/us/35b.asp

The Origins of the Republican Party. 2013. Retrieved November 14, 2014, from http://www.ushistory.org/gop/origins.htm

Why Four Justices Were Against the Supreme Court's Huge Gay-Marriage Decision. 2015, June 26. Retrieved July 29, 2015, from http://www.nationaljournal.com/domesticpolicy/marriage-same-sex-gay-supreme-court-dissent-20150626

www.independentsentinel.com. 2015. Retrieved July 29, 2015, from http://www.independentsentinel.com/obama-grovels-before-castro-as-raul-demeans-the-

Ertelt, S. (2015). Hillary Clinton: Force Christians to Change Their Religious Views to Support Abortion. Retrieved June 30, 2016, from http://www.lifenews.com/2015/04/27/hillary-clinton-force-christians-to-change-their-religious-views-to-support-abortion/

Farah, J. (2016). Who Was the First Birther. Retrieved from http://www.wnd.com/2016/09/who-was-the-first-birther/

Hunter, D. (2014). Michelle To Black Voters: Just Vote Democrat, Then Celebrate With Fried Chicken. Retrieved from http://dailycaller.com/2014/11/04/michelle-obamas-closing-argument-to-black-voters-dont-think-vote-for-democrats/

www.ingramcontent.com/pod-product-compliance
Lightning Source LLC
Chambersburg PA
CBHW031156270326
41931CB00006B/290